CIVILITY UNBOUND

Edited by
Michael F. DiNiscia
and Ellyn M. Toscano

CONTESTING A DEMOCRATIC VALUE

Un

Civility bound

New York University Press New York

NEW YORK UNIVERSITY PRESS
New York
www.nyupress.org

Please contact the Library of Congress for Cataloging-in-Publication data.

ISBN: 9781479840496 (hardback)
ISBN: 9781479842162 (paperback)
ISBN: 9781479840526 (library ebook)
ISBN: 9781479840519 (consumer ebook)

This book is printed on acid-free paper, and its binding materials are chosen for strength and durability. We strive to use environmentally responsible suppliers and materials to the greatest extent possible in publishing our books.

The manufacturer's authorized representative in the EU for product safety is Mare Nostrum Group B.V., Mauritskade 21D, 1091 GC Amsterdam, The Netherlands. Email: gpsr@mare-nostrum.co.uk.

Manufactured in the United States of America

10 9 8 7 6 5 4 3 2 1

Also available as an ebook

For my grandmother, who by her constant example taught me the meaning of civility, and for my nephew and nieces, who I know will make the world more civil for us all
Michael F. DiNiscia

For my mother, for "bringing the gifts that my ancestors gave," and for my daughter, who will carry them forward with determination and courage. Each is a source of hope and strength
(Maya Angelou, "Still I Rise")
Ellyn M. Toscano

Contents

Introduction

MICHAEL F. DINISCIA AND ELLYN M. TOSCANO

We live in a moment when it seems that our politics, our society, even our personal relationships are riven by ever-deepening strife. Our nation is becoming more and more heterogeneous, yet polarizing along partisan lines virtually straight down the middle. It feels as if conflict is rising exponentially, on social media and in daily social interactions, from campuses to Capitol Hill. Heated rhetoric dominates. Civil discourse and compromise seem further and further out of reach. And it's all taking an increasing toll on our communities and culture, even our friendships and families.

How did we get here? What might it take to pull us out of this quagmire of incivility affecting so many aspects of our lives?

For inspiration in tackling this challenge, we looked to the legacy of John Brademas. A longtime member of Congress and president of New York University, John founded a public policy center at NYU that bears his name and with which we are both affiliated. We were particularly struck by an essay he wrote for a 2011 book entitled *Civility in America*.[1] The volume, featuring contributions from John Brademas and other leaders in media, business, and politics, included a surprising epigraph, a quote from Joshua Lederberg, a molecular biologist and winner of the 1958 Nobel Prize in Medicine: "All of civility depends on being able to contain the rage of individuals."

This sentiment seemed an appropriate starting point for our own inquiry, the right framework for evaluating the purchase of civility in contemporary society. Perhaps an examination of civility could originate only in an acknowledgment of the pervasive and pernicious rage that characterizes our times (even if it has been worse at other junctures in our history). And so we began by looking at all the compelling reasons to call for civility in the public square, reasons having to do with the need to preserve democracy, facilitate dialogue among diverse perspectives, encourage solutions to seemingly intractable problems, govern better, indeed contain raging passions.

Yet we quickly came to see how civility is a contested value, deeply complicated by questions of power and control. Civility as a virtue is contested precisely *because* it seeks to contain rage and may therefore silence the outrage that needs to be heard. Can civility both contain the rage of individuals and ensure that the justified cause of their rage is acknowledged and respected? In her contribution to this volume, the renowned feminist scholar Catharine Stimpson insists: "If one is harmed, one must have the ability to speak about it and be heard."

A number of scholars have tackled this dichotomy in their work on the theory and practice of civility. Whether they approach it from political science, sociology, law, communications, or philosophy, we are indebted to scholars such as Stephen Carter of Yale, Linda McClain of Boston University, and Olúfẹmi O. Táíwò of Georgetown who have examined the evolution of civility, its rules and their enforcement, and its utility for us today. And we are immensely grateful to have been able to engage for our inquiry here other leading academics who have contributed a great deal to this field, including social psychologist Jonathan Haidt, scholar of literature and gender studies Lynn Mie Itagaki, and sociologist Sarah Sobieraj.

John Brademas charged the NYU Brademas Center with the mission of "bringing together thinkers and doers." For this volume we have assembled a remarkable group of writers to examine the concept of civility and whether it has value in our contemporary society or is, instead, an anachronism no longer relevant to our public life. Some of the essayists here, such as Jonathan Haidt, Lynn Mie Itagaki, and Sarah Sobieraj, are known for their profound explorations of civility. Others are incredibly thoughtful scholars we asked to take on the topic, who offer up new perspectives. In addition, we've brought in practitioners like union leader Larry Cohen, former member of Congress Mickey Edwards, and poet Ricardo Maldonado to share from their experiences what civility means.

The essays you will find here range from academic research pieces to more personal reflections. All of them bring a wealth of scholarship and experience to bear on the topic. We hope that such an examination—from the fields of history, political science, philosophy, sociology, arts, and communications as well as views from leaders in government and civil society—has the potential to get to the heart of the utility and limits of civility today.

We charged our writers with five topics under the theme of civility. The journey begins with an interrogation of civility in which essayists address such questions as: What are the possibilities and limits of civility? Whom does its exercise benefit? Whom does it silence or harm?

The second section focuses on civility in the political realm, an arena of particular relevance in the beginning decades of the 21st century. We ask: How important is the practice of civility in guiding political debate and behavior? What role does it play in the proper functioning of our political institutions, in policy outcomes, and in the protection of democratic norms?

The third section attempts to locate the place of civility in efforts to achieve social goals, such as racial justice and equality. In this context—confronting the status quo or trying to bring about societal change—the concept of civility can be complex. For example, are calls for civility and civil discourse merely an excuse to ask people to remain silent or polite in the face of injustice? What separates civil from uncivil disobedience?

The fourth section confronts a possible culprit in the erosion of civility: advances in technology and particularly the rise of social media combined with the decline of local and community-based news sources. And here comes AI barreling down the road. Are we now in a place where the loudest and angriest and cruelest—and most untrustworthy—among us control the floor?

The final section looks for lessons on civility from those beyond the usual suspects—namely, perspectives informed by popular culture, storytelling, poetry, and the arts, even comedy. What can we learn from these vantage points about how to navigate conflict, embrace differences, and create community?

A Democratic Virtue?

Several ideas and lessons surfaced from the essays. A number of writers trace the etymology of civility and its relationship to citizenship. The philosopher Anthony Appiah begins with a discussion of the rights that came with being a Roman citizen: *civis Romanus*. "Those civil, citizen's, rights were quite extensive and complex," and "what comes with the 'civil' is a very wide range of norms and commitments." Civility, then, is a notion related to status, honor, and privilege. It refers to the reciprocal obligations citizens owe to each other *as citizens*, and by extension to the state. Appiah notes that this connection to ideals of citizenship does not get us very far in distilling a definition of civility. Catharine Stimpson concurs: "As an ideal and social practice, civility carries a lot of baggage."

Civility is frequently invoked, nostalgically, in reference to an undefined time of past social cohesion. In this context, it is frequently paired with manners and the decorum required to ensure peaceful interactions in the public square. Yet, as Stimpson reminds us, "historically, it defined the active citizen—when active citizenship might be limited to one class, gender, or race. . . . [It] defined the cultured person—when ideas of culture might be limited to one nation, race, or group. Finally, civility has defined the polite person, the well-mannered person—when politesse and good manners might be the deceptive public performance of someone who is impolite, badly mannered, even brutal and hypocritical in private." Civility, Lynne Mie Itagaki writes in her essay, is "both deceptively expansive and restrictive."

Many of the essays examine the role partisan politics plays in the decline of civility, given the perceived dramatic deterioration of the quality of public debate and abandonment of norms of political discourse long thought enshrined, or universally accepted, in American political life. But, as John Brademas warned in his 2011 essay in *Civility in America,* we should not look "longingly back to a time when politics was marked by its civility, because we risk becoming nostalgic for a more civil time that may never have really existed." Indeed, the political scientist Julia Azari recounts in her essay robust rhetorical attacks that were part and parcel of 19th century American presidential campaigns.

Despite this history, can civility's relationship to citizenship help us think of it as a public value, related to mutual responsibilities and obligations of respect? Can we see civility as a democratic and pluralistic imperative, helping us set some ground rules for managing social and political conflict in a context of widely diverse viewpoints? Mickey Edwards argues persuasively that, notwithstanding the obvious "strain on attempts to forge common purpose," civility is not "just 'niceness' or 'good manners' or 'tolerance.' It's something deeper. It's respect—respect for the humanity of even those with whom we disagree most ardently and are most determined to defeat. It's a shared openness—at least a willingness to listen without simultaneously forming a rebuttal; not just listening, but hearing. And it's restraint. Not every thought that pops into your head needs to come shooting out of your mouth."

Jonathan Haidt argues that civility, even in a "minimal form," is necessary in a functioning liberal democracy. Focusing his attention on the "rampant incivility" of social media that "supercharges moralistic anger while dissolving trust and cooperation," Haidt declares that "when the response to an argument is an effort to damage the speaker's reputation, social standing, or employment, then the chilling effect on speech is similar to the effect of threats of violence." He continues: "Without a widely shared commitment to civil disagreement . . . internal dissent diminishes or disappears, and the institutions of liberal democracy malfunction." His definition of civility then, is framed, in part, as a negative obligation, "a commitment to refrain from attempting to harm those with whom we disagree." Catharine Stimpson proposes that civility "can offer a set of norms for political and social relations that reject the infliction of suffering. If enough people behave in accord with these norms, more caring and lively communities will emerge." These norms, which she describes as "the new decorum," are aspirations around which we can surely coalesce.

Understanding that conflict and debate can be generative and progressive, civility can help us think about the norms of discourse and expression of difference, even difference of values. Larry Cohen discusses the importance of civility and the rules of debate *within* movements for social and labor rights: "Social justice movements need a combination of mass organizing; protest, including civil disobedience; and electoral and political action. Mass organizing, as with union organizing, requires internal civility, treating participants with equal respect and listening more than talking. Protest similarly requires civility internally and externally, or the message is obscured. Nonviolence in thought as well as action is an essential element of civil disobedience."

Caty Borum, both a scholar and practitioner of comedy, wonderfully draws lessons from that field for ways we might reach mutual respect. "How can we find new ways to encourage ourselves and others to learn, feel, and engage with people, lived realities, and social problems that may not be our own, or about which we disagree?" She offers an answer: "Through comedy, we open a portal to see our flaws and absurdity, and thus, our shared humanity. And it is in these small spaces where we can find one another."

Lastly, Anthony Appiah maintains that civility requires a willingness to compromise: "We need a form of civility—a disposition toward each other as fellow-citizens—that seeks practical compromises rather than ideological triumph."

Civility and Power

As a concept connoting agreement to rules of debate, a framework for comprehending and negotiating difference, a means of harnessing disagreement and engaging with opposition, many of our contributors argue for the value of civility. Others, however, raise serious challenges to its utility.

Perhaps civility is irrelevant when the struggle is for justice and the rebalance of power in a world that views power as a zero-sum struggle, seems to no longer value truth, and privileges fear over reason. Lynn Itagaki contends that "civility rarely helps balance the voices of the strong and weak, but is instead a weapon of the wealthy and powerful." Is it not true that "both our present and our past history about social change, about protest, about mass political action demonstrate to us time and again that civility is simply the card that those in power play when masses of people threaten that power," as the scholar of racial justice and digital media Charlton McIlwain asserts? Or, as Hussein Rashid, an expert in religion and public life, describes the structure of power implicit in civility, that "civility, as a state, is the enforcement of social power structures and hierarchies. That enforcement is carried out by those in power, who treat violations of civility as a rationale for the discipline of the powerless."

Lynn Itagaki points out that the division between *civilis,* "of or pertaining to citizens," and *incivilitas,* "not for citizens," established this power dynamic. "This division," she writes, "may seem obvious on paper and in abstraction; however, divisions between citizens and noncitizens have been invoked to justify and trigger unrestrained, legally sanctioned brutalities—the worst of which are now considered crimes against humanity. Even if legal restrictions have been loosened over time, the descendants or perceived descendants of those who were once noncitizens continue to face the bigotry resulting from the incivility of their presumed illegitimate and undeserved citizenship." She describes how this divide empowers the groups who benefit from the status quo to delegitimize actors who challenge it: "Incivility is usually understood as a rupture of a perceived norm or past status quo: a rude comment or gesture, anger or raised voices that are surprising; groups of people gathering, marching, or occupying spaces that are not customarily used in these ways; or physical force or violence where none has occurred or been acknowledged before." We need look no further than the expulsion in 2023 of two Democratic lawmakers in Tennessee for their protest on the floor of the legislature. They were calling for more gun safety legislation in the aftermath of a deadly school shooting in Nashville. The resolution of expulsion cited the two for "disorderly behavior"; the action was taken because the members violated "several rules of decorum," in the words of the House speaker.[2]

Is civility even possible in our politics, when it feels as if truth, justice, and respect are assailed or disregarded virtues? Longtime scholar of Congress Norm Ornstein is pessimistic. He lays out the recent history of increasing incivility on Capitol Hill beginning with the rise of Newt Gingrich and his no-holds-barred approach to electoral politics. Ornstein describes the degradation of political norms and practices leading to "tribalization." In the end, he warns that with the hostility to truth and consensus that characterizes contemporary political discourse, with social media spreading lies and seeking to "divide people and inflame judgments, we find ourselves in an extremely difficult place."

Redeeming Civility

If civility is important, it is because it can be the instantiation of human empathy. It should serve the function of providing the guardrails in the battle among ideas and resolution of difference. It can provide us with goals and values to which to aspire as a society. It could, for example, through comedy, help us constitute the new "civic imagination" as suggested by Caty Borum, bringing us to "a shared cultural understanding." It could be, in the words of Catharine Stimpson, "a call for the dissolution of the cruelties of our species, which run the gamut from loutish stupidities to the application of sophisticated braininess, and for the growth of a virtuous wisdom—before it is too late."

Hussein Rashid warns of the difficulty in redeeming civility as a value. "Without the recognition of how civility is weaponized," he argues, "it cannot be recovered to serve as a space to bring citizens together. As Americans, we need to understand how we can participate in debate, dialogue, and disagreement in ways that result in productive and generative resolution. Civility, as it stands now, hastens polarization and division. Parties cannot engage with one another as long as the implicit starting point by one of the parties is the preservation of current power systems."

Is it civility or is it truth that is essential for engagement across difference and respect for disagreement? And what is civility without truth? What can be expected of civility in a toxic climate that the Center for Countering Digital Hate founder Imran Ahmed describes is being fostered by angry online content and "non-falsifiable statements that cannot be disproved"? Ahmed asserts that "disinformation is the ultimate example of incivility." And what of justice when we find ourselves living in a system we created for ourselves that incentivizes conflict and controversy? The journalist Paul Cheung explains how, in the chase for advertising dollars, our 24–7 television and online news media elevates the angriest voices in order to drive viewership and engagement.

If your interlocutor, while admonishing you for your supposed incivility, is himself not constrained by respect for truth or moral instinct toward justice, what does civility even mean? Isn't civility, then, an empty gesture? Poet Ricardo Maldonado reaches this conclusion. He writes: "Truth informs our shared obligations. That may be, on my end, the only project that may ring true for me, at any rate, sustaining the prosody of the medium itself. Not the performance of civility, merely, but mutual regard, a strong obligation."

While questioning the validity of a remembered civil past, John Brademas hoped that an examination of civility could make a contribution to our thoughts about contemporary discourse. As he wrote in his 2011 essay, "While there may be no golden age of civility in politics, perhaps we can still learn some lessons from how, even during periods of tragedy, division, and conflict in American society and politics, leaders could still find common ground and identity and work together on important issues." This, then, is the challenge we gave to our contributors.

We see this collection as the start of a discussion, with its multidisciplinary approach offering differing viewpoints and ideas. The essays propose varied visions of civility—many overlapping, some competing—all in a conversation with one another. We hope they will illuminate such a contested and challenging topic. We also hope they will provide new paths of inquiry for researchers and students, as Sarah Sobieraj calls for "input from other scholars concerned about the political climate and information environment in the US. . . . Together we can develop the tools we need to recognize and interrogate attempts to manufacture institutional distrust, as such weaponization efforts have proven electorally expedient and are likely to continue."

We should also not give in to despair about the decline of empathy in our politics and respect in our discourse. We can take heart from lessons from our actual shared, not nostalgically imagined, past, as Karen Jackson-Weaver shows with examples from the Civil Rights Movement. As polarized as politics and society feel now, we have faced difficult times throughout our nation's history and risen to the challenge.

In the end, civility has a value that is nonquantifiable and aspirational, reflecting how we want our public life to be conducted. But it is not the only value. Civility must serve, not suppress, other values and norms fundamental to public life, especially an unwavering, foundational commitment to truth and dedication to justice.

NOTES

1 Robert L. Dilenschneider, ed., *Civility in America* (DGI, 2011).

2 Nadine Yousif, Brandon Drenon, and Melisa Goh, "Lawmakers Expelled: What to Know About the 'Tennessee Three,'" BBC, April 7, 2023, www.bbc.com.

PART I

Interrogating Civility

1

Civility

Moral Powers and Conversations Across Difference

K. ANTHONY APPIAH

Because "civility" has its root in a Latin word for a citizen, it's natural to think the term implies a disposition to treat other citizens appropriately. When St. Paul insisted that he and Silas were Romans, he was reminding the magistrates of Philippi that, in beating and imprisoning them, they had violated the rights that came with being a *civis Romanus*. And, as the King James Bible puts it, the magistrates "feared, when they heard that they were Romans." (Acts 16:38) Those civil, citizen's, rights were quite extensive and complex. John Austin, the great English legal philosopher, observes in his *Lectures on Jurisprudence*, "The word civil has about twelve different meanings; it is applied to all manner of objects, which are perfectly disparate."[1] What comes with the "civil" is a very wide range of norms and commitments.

If you take the Greek word for a citizen, "πολίτης" (polités), as your root instead, you get "polite," and one job of "civility" is indeed to refer to a baseline of good manners between citizens. Manners are important.[2] Unless they have wronged us, strangers deserve to be treated with respect. That's basic morality. And the conventions of manners determine what sorts of behavior count, in a particular society, as showing that consideration. Refusing a proffered hand counts in our society as a snub . . . absent a good reason of the kind we may have during the pandemic not to touch other people's hands, an explanation that needs to be given to avoid reasonable offense. In Japan, courtesy requires you, other things once more being equal, to bow.

But more is at stake here than manners.

In a democracy, we are each equally charged with piloting the ship of state together. When we relate *as* fellow-citizens, we should treat each other respectfully, not as a matter of manners, but because we actually *regard* each other with genuine respect. Who could be more worthy of respect than someone who is engaged with you in that important shared task?

This demand can be a problem in a society as diverse as ours. John Rawls proposed a solution, starting from what he called our "two moral powers": our *sense of justice,* which guides each to offer fair terms of cooperation to the others; and our *conception of the good,* our ideas about what it is for a human life to go well.[3] That sense of justice is central, because we each have *different* conceptions of the good life. And that circumstance sets the challenge for finding fair terms of cooperation. If we all agreed on what was the best life—a life of Christian service, a life of submission to Allah, an Epicurean philosophy of carpe diem—we could converge on an idea of society that enabled such a life. But Rawls recognized that a modern society must proceed without any such agreement.

North Atlantic liberals came slowly to that understanding as a result of the disastrous European wars of religion that followed the Reformation. It turned out you couldn't convert people at the point of the sword. And the practical reality that it was impossible to enforce agreement was eventually accompanied by an ethical idea: that people were entitled to live by their own ideals. This powerful conception was articulated forcefully by John Stuart and Harriet Mill in *On Liberty*: your life is centrally for you to manage, and you are entitled to live according to your own conception of what is good. I have long loved these words from chapter 3 of *On Liberty*: "If a person possesses any tolerable amount of common sense and experience, his own mode of laying out his existence is the best, not because it is the best in itself, but because it is his own mode."[4]

John Locke's anticipations of liberalism in his *First Treatise of Government* responded to Filmer's *Patriarcha or the Natural Right of Kings,* which derived political authority from the "natural" authority of the father. If you are a child under the control of a traditional patriarch, he gets to determine what life is best for you; he has the authority to command it. But in a liberal democracy, each of us can say to the others, "You're not the boss of me." As a consequence, politics is a matter of managing our common life on terms of equality, terms that have to suit us all.

John Rawls's *Political Liberalism* is clearer than Mill that there are constraints on what conceptions of the good life we must respect. They must be what he called reasonable. Part of what makes a view reasonable is that it acknowledges the difficulty of disputes about these matters, and so allows that other people who disagree with us about them need not be viewed by us as confused or biased or selfish. All of that, though, is consistent with a pretty wide range of conceptions of the good; which, as I say, makes setting fair terms of cooperation harder.[5]

These ideas will fail to impress many of our fellow citizens today, especially if we tell them that these are the core ideas of liberalism, since many seem to think that liberalism is precisely what they abhor. But unless they are ready to contemplate policies of expulsion or extermination, they are bound, if they are reasonable, to agree that we need to figure out how to live together with our different ideas about how to live well. We can argue about the limits of the reasonable, but they are bound to have to consider Rawls's question about what makes for fair terms of cooperation among reasonable people.

And, once they see that question, they must accept (again, if they are reasonable) that we have to be able to discuss these issues, despite our differences, and that our conversations will lead nowhere if they are always angry and discourteous. Civility as politeness arises within a liberal vision; but it is also a piece of practical good sense. I don't mean we can never raise our voices. Sometimes, when someone has wronged you, indignation is appropriate, and you *should* raise your voice. Outrage sometimes communicates better the strength of a conviction or the depth of a wrong. But we cannot shout all the time; we won't find routes to cooperation and to compromise if we never lower our voices. Sometimes, to insist on the point, civility requires politeness.

But, once more, courtesy cannot be enough.

We have problems to solve together. We need a form of civility—a disposition toward each other as fellow-citizens—that seeks practical compromises rather than ideological triumph. I must be willing to accept solutions that do not seem to me the best when they make it easier for others to accept them, too.[6] One thing civility requires beyond politeness is a willingness to compromise. And what is often referred to as our current ideological "tribalism" is making that impossible.

• • •

My own understanding of what's wrong with tribalism comes from a particular political background, far away from this country I have now chosen as my own. Despite that distance, it continues to provide me with a powerful model for thinking about what we owe one another as citizens. At the turn of the 1950s, my father campaigned in Britain for Ghanaian independence, representing Kwame Nkrumah, our first president; and he was elected to our first parliament in the late 1950s. He loved our country: his autobiography is called *Joe Appiah: The Autobiography of an African Patriot*. He was born, though, in Kumasi, in the British Crown

Colony of Ashanti, the capital of what had once been the Asante Empire, where my grandfather had been, in effect, the prime minister of the Asante king. My dad, like *his* father, had a strong sense of identity as an Asante. And Ashanti became formally part of Ghana only at independence.

One of the great themes of my father's life over the next 30 years, as a democratic Ghanaian politician born into an Asante ruling class, was the importance of resisting what he called "tribalism."

In Ghanaian English, we call our many ethnic groups "tribes," and most Ghanaians will eagerly tell you their tribe if you ask. Ghana has 23 languages that are spoken by more than 50,000 people; there are 80 or more languages altogether, some spoken by more than one tribe. Depending on how you count, we've at least a hundred tribes.

One thing you could mean by the word "tribalism" is being overinvested in these older political identities (older, that is, than Ghana) and not giving proper weight to the modern national identity as a result. My father thought that when you were acting as a national politician—in the Ghanaian Parliament, say—you shouldn't seek unfair advantage for your tribe over the others; and you should never fail to give proper weight to the concerns of tribes other than your own. This was an ideal that our politics has never fully lived up to: everybody has always been fully aware of the tribal origins of Ghana's political leaders, and everyone supposes that there can be unwarranted advantages in being a fellow member of a presidential ethnic group. But the ideal is important, nevertheless: political cultures are defined by such ideals, even when we don't live up to them. The state is not meant to have a tribal identity. That's the ideal that anti-tribalism stands for. Ghana is meant not to be Asante in the way that many (though, alas, not all) Americans believe the United States is meant not to be Christian or White.[7] It isn't meant to be Republican or Democrat, liberal or conservative, either. It is meant to be a country we can all honor and love.

• • •

What, then, is to be done?

Long ago, the psychologist Gordon Allport argued that contact between individuals of different identities makes hostility less likely if it occurs in a framework that meets certain conditions: crucially, it must be on terms of rough equality and in activities where shared goals are pursued in ways that demand reliance on one another.[8] America's racially integrated armed services, for example, produce people who are less racist, on average, when they leave than when they arrive. But our political tribes are increasingly segregated. We need to find more spaces where people of our dominant political tribes build the social trust that allows all tribes to cohabit. We need to be in conversation with one another across our differences.

Here's a kind of just-so story, an illuminating fiction that carries an important truth. It exemplifies how that kind of conversation across difference can work. In an episode of the TV series *Skins*, about a group of high-school students in England, there's a birthday party for Anwar, an English teenager of South Asian ancestry, whose father is a devout Muslim. Anwar's best friend, Maxxie, unlike Anwar, is gay. And he's been waiting for Anwar to tell his parents, which Anwar has been scared to do. So Maxxie is standing outside, refusing to come into the party until Anwar finally tells them. While the boys are talking, Anwar's father comes out. He tells Maxxie that Mrs. Kharral has prepared a spicy curry for him, a spicy lamb bhuna that she knows he loves. He asks Maxxie why he's not coming in. As he and Maxxie talk, Anwar finally says, "Dad, Maxxie's gay." His father ignores him. Then Maxxie himself says, "I'm gay, Mr. Kharral. I always have been." There's a long silence. Anwar waits anxiously in the background to hear what his father will say. And then Mr. Kharral says this: "It's a . . . stupid, messed-up world. I've got my God; he speaks to me every day. Some things I just can't work out. So, I leave them be, okay, even if I think they're wrong. Because I know, one day, He'll make me understand. I've got that trust. It's called belief. I'm a lucky man. Right? Come, Maxxie, the food's ready."[9]

This is how things are with people who are in conversation with one another. Mr. Kharral belongs to the Muslim tribe; Maxxie's tribe is Christian or, perhaps, post-Christian. But they don't need to agree. They have only to accept each other. And they can do that without shared principles, because being together has generated commitments that can transcend even serious disagreement. We need to find places across the tribes to build such social capital.

Mr. Kharral begins in exactly the right place. The world is hard to understand, and he may not be right about everything. He doesn't forsake his belief that homosexuality is wrong: he puts it aside as something to work out later. Right now, what matters is celebrating his son's 17th birthday with his son's best friend. This works in practice. It doesn't need a theory.

I am a philosopher. I *like* theories. But if we are to treat each other properly as fellow citizens, theory isn't the only thing that matters.

NOTES

1 John Austin, *Lectures on Jurisprudence: The Philosophy of Positive Law* (John Murray, 1873), end of lecture 44.

2 I rather like the motto of my grandfather's school, Winchester, and my great-grandfather's Oxford college, New College, which was the personal code of William of Wykeham, a 14th-century bishop of Winchester, who founded them both: "Manners," he said, "makyth man."

3 "The basic idea is that in virtue of their two moral powers (a capacity for a sense of justice and for a conception of the good) and the powers of reason (of judgment, thought, and inference connected with these powers),

persons are free." John Rawls, *Political Liberalism* (Columbia University Press, 1996), 19.

4 John Stuart Mill, *On Liberty* in *The Collected Works of John Stuart Mill*, ed. John M. Robson (University of Toronto Press, 1963–91), 18:270.

5 Rawls was pretty generous about the variety of views he meant to allow and certainly took most modern religious traditions to fall within range: "The only comprehensive doctrines that run afoul of public reason on a given question are those that cannot support a reasonable balance of political values" (*Political Liberalism*, 243).

6 I am one of those liberals who, in Robert Frost's famous jibe, cannot take his own side in an argument.

7 In a Public Religion Research Institute survey in 2020, 36 percent of Americans surveyed said that "the United States has always been and is currently a Christian nation." Public Religion Research Institute, "Amid Multiple Crises, Trump and Biden Supporters See Different Realities and Futures for the Nation," October 19, 2020, www.prri.org.

8 Gordon Allport, *The Nature of Prejudice* (Basic Books, 1979).

9 Skins, "When You Come Out as Gay to Your Friends [*sic*] Dad," YouTube video, 1:57, November 5, 2008, www.youtube.com.

2

The Kind of Civility That Liberal Institutions Need to Survive

JONATHAN HAIDT

I'd like to approach the topic of civility by telling a story about the rise and fall of liberal institutions and, perhaps, liberal societies. The story will illustrate why liberal societies require a certain kind of civility. I don't mean civility as politeness and decorum. In a robust democracy, there is a role for anger and protest and norm violation, and even at times civil disobedience. There will always be wide disagreements about what constitutes politeness and rudeness in a culturally diverse society.

I would like to suggest instead a very low bar—a minimal form of civility we must have in a functioning liberal democracy. I mean civility as a commitment to refrain from attempting to harm those with whom we disagree. Physical harm and threats of violence are, of course, illegal as well as uncivil, but I'd like to expand the realm of impermissible harm to include social and financial harm. It's fine to say publicly that someone's argument is wrong, deluded, hypocritical, or even stupid. (Calling someone stupid *can* damage reputation, whereas calling an argument stupid may not.) But when the response to an argument is an effort to damage the speaker's reputation, social standing, or employment, then the chilling effect on speech is similar to the effect of threats of violence.

Without a widely shared commitment to civil disagreement defined in this way, internal dissent diminishes or disappears, and the institutions of liberal democracy malfunction. I will argue that since the early 2010s, social media has caused a tidal wave of reputational attacks and hence incivility, and, as a result, many of the key institutions of America's liberal democracy are now malfunctioning, badly.

The Rise of Liberal Epistemic Institutions

Once upon a time, there was no good way to find the truth on matters of science, history, and public policy. There were people offering conjectures, and there were religious leaders consulting sacred texts. But in the 17th century, according to Jonathan Rauch, a scholar at the Brookings Institution, Western societies began developing effective epistemic—or knowledge-creating—institutions. In *The Constitution of Knowledge,* Rauch explores the origins of these institutions, which made it possible to generate ever-better approximations of truth from the conflicting beliefs and motivations of individuals who were not, themselves, particularly good at finding truth.[1] An example of such an epistemic institution is the early coffeeshops in London and Paris, where men interested in science met to discuss the latest artifacts brought back by explorers, or the latest theories published in a book or inexpensive pamphlet.

Over time, these communities turned into today's scientific communities, based partly but not entirely at universities—and one of the coffeeshops became the Royal Society for the Arts. Similar evolutions took place in journalism, as the low standards of the penny press and "yellow journalism" turned into the profession of journalism, with editors, fact checkers, and trade associations that confer awards for journalistic excellence. Similar evolutions took place in legal systems, which developed better norms and rules for finding truth from the adversarial interactions of the parties in a dispute.

Rauch's compelling metaphor is that these constellations of people, norms, and institutions do not just "constitute" knowledge, in the sense of creating it; they are also a kind of "constitution of knowledge," analogous to the US Constitution as designed by James Madison. Both, says Rauch, are ingenious systems that harness disagreement and turn it into knowledge, policy, and progress. Individuals enter a discussion, debate, or contest with differing cherished beliefs, which they try hard to confirm, never to disconfirm. If the institution is set up well, then the confirmation biases cancel each other out. Each participant is motivated to find the counterevidence that her opponent cannot dig up for himself.

This constitution of knowledge reached its pinnacle in the United States in the mid-to-late 20th century, a period when the United States and its universities were the most productive in the world, and when its private and public corporations excelled at creating new knowledge and commercializing new scientific discoveries. Scientists, engineers, corporations, and government agencies worked together to perform a miracle that, arguably, has not yet been surpassed. In 1969, in an era of slide rules and primitive computers, they put Americans on the moon.

There never was a Camelot—a perfect time when American institutions all worked gloriously—but there are now clear signs that something is going wrong in the 21st century. Trust in institutions is down, including trust in the epistemic institutions of journalism and universities (particularly among those on the political right).[2] Affective polarization (hatred of people on the other side) is up, and the ability of the US Congress to pass important legislation in the past 15 years seems to be confined to the occasional two-year period when one party controls both chambers and the presidency.[3] All of this was true before Donald Trump became president, and then things got much worse, with no sign of improvement since he left.

The Solvent of Social Media

Changes in technology create pivot points in history, often after a delay. Changes in communication technology are particularly potent, especially when they go beyond changing the way information flows to alter the nature of social relationships. I am a social psychologist who studies morality, and I have come to believe that social media—at least, the subset of platforms whose business model incentivizes users to generate free content that can "go viral" to draw in other users so that the platform can sell ads—has fundamentally changed social relations in a way that supercharges moralistic anger while dissolving trust and cooperation. In doing so, social media has had a notably devastating impact on the institutions that comprise the "constitution of knowledge." If those institutions fail, then so will liberal democracy.

Social media was relatively harmless in its early incarnations, around 2004. Platforms such as Myspace, Friendster, and Facebook made it easy for people to post information about themselves, and to see what their friends, colleagues, and favorite bands posted about themselves. Its benign impact began to change in 2009, when Facebook introduced the "like" button. With reams of new data about which posts "engaged" users, Facebook then developed algorithms that would preferentially feed people whatever posts caused them to click. Later research showed that anger is among the most "engaging" features of a post.[4] Also in 2009, Twitter introduced the "retweet" button, which Facebook copied as its "share" button.

These changes, which were rolled out widely across other platforms over the next few years, transformed the dynamics of social media into a new world governed by power laws and exponential possibilities. The metaphor of "virality" is a very close match to the dynamics of social media. As we all learned during the COVID pandemic, a small change to one parameter (such as Ro—the variable expressing the transmissibility of a viral strain) can have an enormous effect on the number of people who die.

Chris Wetherel, an engineer at Twitter who helped to develop the retweet button, later came to regret his participation. Watching Twitter mobs form, he thought to himself, "We must have just handed a 4-year-old a loaded weapon."[5] But let's modify his metaphor, since mean tweets don't kill anyone; they just bring shame and social or reputational damage. Instead, let's think about Twitter and Facebook as having passed out dart guns, which could be used freely to attack anyone, anywhere, often anonymously, without having to worry about evidence, context, nuance, truth, or due process. This, I believe, is the key change that the newly viralized social media platforms wrought in the 2010s: they gave little dart guns to everyone. They democratized intimidation and freed it from accountability.

The emergent consequence was not more responsible behavior by the leaders of institutions; it was rampant incivility. Anyone could publicly shame or slander anyone else—even call for the person to lose his or her job—and face no consequences for lies or misrepresentation. This new and widespread fear of social attacks for good-faith speech has had catastrophic effects on American institutions since the mid-2010s.

The Betrayal of Institutional Telos

What happens to a society when everyone carries a dart gun? Just imagine how your speech would change if you knew that at any moment, strangers who overheard your conversation could shoot a dart into your arm if they felt at all offended. After getting darted a few times, you'd change the way you talk, as surely as an animal learns to modify its behavior when strong electric shocks are administered in a behaviorist experiment. You'd be careful. You'd act as though you lived in a mine field, or were walking on eggshells. You'd self-censor like mad.

And what if you were leading an epistemic institution?

At this point in the story, I'd like to introduce a helpful concept for analyzing the sudden collapse of America's epistemic institutions in the late 2010s: *telos*, the ancient Greek word for "end" or "purpose." In *The Physics*, Aristotle says that when we want to explain causation, we ask four questions, the fourth being: Why was the thing done? For what telos (end or purpose)?

All professions have a telos, by which we can judge whether a member of the profession is good or bad. The telos of a physician is health or healing. A doctor who cannot heal others is a bad doctor.[6] When we ask, "Why did the doctor make this diagnosis?" or, "Why did the doctor prescribe this drug?" the answer had better be, "Because she was trying to heal her patient." It had better not be, "Because that drug company pays her a larger kickback than if she had prescribed the generic drug."

Of course, the doctor needs to earn money to support her practice, her staff, and her family, but if she allows moneymaking to become her telos, rather than a secondary goal, and if she gives inferior care to her patients to make more money for herself, then we can say that she has betrayed the telos of the physician. She is a bad doctor, and she should be investigated by her professional society—in this case, the American Medical Association. If the professional society allows such corrupt behavior to spread, then, over time, people will justifiably lose trust in the AMA, in doctors in general, and in their own doctor.

We can conduct the same sort of analysis for the other professions and institutions that are part of the constitution of knowledge. Lawyers strive for justice using the methods of their profession. Researchers, journalists, and accountants all strive for truth using the methods of their professions. All professionals are subject to constraints, safeguards, and oversight as required by their professions. All of them are at risk of corruption if they take on a second telos, such as earning money. In fact, an institution cannot have a second telos. It can have multiple goals or values, which sometimes conflict. But the telos of an institution is more than a value; it is like a north star, an axis around which everything else spins. An institution that tries to rotate around two different north stars will inevitably tear itself apart or descend into dysfunction.

What would happen if there were a political movement that wanted the professions to take on a different telos—let's say, national greatness, or the victory of the proletariat, or fighting communism, or glorifying Christ, or a specific ideology around race—and it was willing to use violence to compel doctors, lawyers, accountants, journalists, and professors to change their procedures and their substantive findings to advance that goal? This is just the sort of heavy-handed pressure that totalitarian regimes have long applied to professionals. It destroys the profession and the public's trust. We assume that Soviet psychiatrists were lying, and certainly not acting in the best interests of their patients, when they diagnosed dissidents as having mental illnesses to justify locking them away.

But is the situation qualitatively different when the threat is not physical violence or imprisonment, but rather reputational destruction? People who are publicly shamed are ostracized, isolated, and often impoverished, since nowadays they are at high risk of losing their jobs and their prospects for finding any future employment. In the internet age, scandals cannot be removed from your résumé. In the ancient world, men and women often chose death before dishonor. In the modern world, adults and adolescents who are publicly shamed sometimes commit suicide.

This is what has happened in most of our key epistemic institutions since around 2015, as America's intensifying culture war was transformed by the arrival of dart guns for everyone. The transformation happened first in America's elite universities, as I wrote with Greg Lukianoff in an article in *The Atlantic* titled "The Coddling of the American Mind."[7] Beginning around 2014, professors and administrators began to discover that a small number of students would react to books, speakers, ideas, and words (very often single words) by claiming not only to be offended but to have been harmed or put in danger.[8] They posted their outrage on social media, thereby putting strong social pressure on the university administration to take action—sometimes an investigation of the speaker, sometimes for the speaker to be fired, sometimes for the administration to accede to a long list of these students' demands. The demands were rarely backed up by reasoned arguments to which counterarguments could be offered; in fact, a hallmark of our current era is that majorities of students now report they are sometimes afraid to say what they believe in class, or on campus, because of the fear of reputational destruction.[9] Many professors report a similar fear.[10]

Some of the reforms that students demanded were illiberal and incompatible with the telos of truth. These included new speech codes, mandatory training sessions with an ideological bent, and new administrative bodies to enforce compliance with a new moral order. I argued, in a 2016 essay, that the students were calling for a new telos for the university: a specific kind of social justice focused on equality of outcomes rather than equality of opportunity.[11] But a university cannot have two conflicting teloses. It cannot orient itself around two different north stars at the same time.

America's epistemic institutions generally lean left, so the dart guns were heavily used by activists on the far left to shoot moderates and leaders within left-leaning institutions. But the far right does now control the Republican Party, and in the new era of mass intimidation, the far right and its allies in purity-enforcing right-wing media have used social media and cable TV to relentlessly attack Republican moderates, most of whom have been driven to retire or beaten into conformity.[12] The Republican party itself has become "structurally stupid" by silencing dissent, and it increasingly countenances extraordinary incivility among its own members, from the rudeness of two conspiracy-obsessed congresswomen who repeatedly heckled President Biden during his first State of the Union Speech[13] to the death threats and harassment of Republican election officials who refused to violate their duties to "stop the steal."[14]

Conclusion

We live at a time when the "culture war" is spreading into ever more domains of life. Some Americans think it is appropriate to shout at public figures in restaurants, or to go to their homes and intimidate their families. Leaders of companies and universities increasingly think they must take sides and broadcast their political sympathies, identifying their organizations as hostile territory for members of the other party. Once a side is taken, the organization generally exhibits zero tolerance for aggression and intimidation toward members of the favored side, while tolerating a high level of aggression and intimidation toward members of the minority or disfavored side—for example, allowing events and visiting speakers favorable to the other side to be shouted down, with no penalty for those doing the shouting.

Civility for me, but not for thee.

When this disequilibrium happens in key epistemic institutions, such as universities, public health agencies, or news agencies that claim to value impartiality, then the constitution of knowledge cannot function. And without a robust constitution of knowledge, then liberal democracy cannot function.

The 21st century began with a great deal of optimism that liberal democracy was destined to triumph over all other forms of government. But by the late 2010s, things looked very different, and it is now clear that we are in for a long struggle between liberal democracies and autocracies. So far, it appears that social media and other forms of digital media are helping China to become a more effective authoritarian state. And so far, social media is making it harder for democracies to be robust and admirable open societies. A basic commitment to the minimum kind of civility I have described is essential if liberal democracy is to prevail.

NOTES

1 Jonathan Rauch, *The Constitution of Knowledge* (Brookings Institution, 2021).

2 See Rebecca Cohen, "Breaking Down Public Trust," University of Michigan Ford School News, fordschool.umich.edu; Rick Edmonds, "US Ranks Last Among 46 Countries in Trust in Media, Reuters Institute Report Finds," Poynter, June 24, 2021, www.poynter.org; and Kim Parker, "The Growing Partisan Divide in Views of Higher Education," Pew Research Center, August 19, 2019, www.pewresearch.org.

3 Rani Molla, "Social Media Is Making a Bad Political Situation Worse," Vox, November 10, 2020, www.vox.com.

4 William J. Brady, Julian A. Wills, John T. Jost, and Jay J. Van Bavel, "Emotion Shapes the Diffusion of Moralized Content In Social Networks," *Proceedings of the National Academy of Sciences* 114, no. 28 (2017): 7313–18.

5 Alex Kantrowitz, "The Man Who Built the Retweet: 'We Handed a Loaded Weapon to 4-Year-Olds,'" BuzzFeed News, July 23, 2019, www.buzzfeednews.com.

6 At least, when we think about prototypes. There are cases peripheral to the prototype, such as a hospice doctor who is trying to reduce suffering rather than produce healing. A doctor who is primarily a researcher has a different telos: discovery of truth.

7 Greg Lukianoff and Jonathan Haidt, "The Coddling of the American Mind," *The Atlantic*, September 2015, www.theatlantic.com.

8 Chris Bodenner, "Now Claremont McKenna," *The Atlantic*, November 12, 2015, www.theatlantic.com.

9 John K. Wilson, "The Inevitable Problem of Self-Censorship," *Inside Higher Ed*, January 11, 2022, www.insidehighered.com.

10 Edward Schlosser, "I'm a Liberal Professor and My Liberal Students Terrify Me," Vox, June 3, 2015, www.vox.com.

11 Jonathan Haidt, "Why Universities Must Choose One Telos: Truth or Social Justice," Heterodox: The Blog, October 21, 2016, https://heterodoxacademy.org.

12 Tim Alberta, "What the GOP Does to Its Own Dissenters," *The Atlantic*, December 7, 2021, www.theatlantic.com.

13 Jordan Mendoza, "Laruen Boebert and Marjorie Taylor Greene Heckle Biden During State of the Union," *USA Today*, March 1, 2022, www.usatoday.com.

14 Michael Wines, "Harassed and Harangued, Poll Workers Now Have a New Form of Defense," *New York Times*, September 18, 2021, www.nytimes.com.

3

The Incivility of Civility*

LYNN MIE ITAGAKI

Primarily thought of as politeness, civility is touted for fostering the mutual respect and turn-taking that increase social cohesion and reciprocity. This essay identifies less the specific behaviors and interactions of civility that might facilitate democratic deliberation to focus more on the unacknowledged or tacit work civility is expected to do: equalize unequal situations.

Civility is often perceived as the precondition for democratic deliberation and thus necessary for achieving equality. It seems to lay the groundwork for such deliberation by enabling negotiations over allocating opportunities and resources to be conducted in a fair and just manner. According to this view, debates over civility represent different ways for people to understand and behave toward each other to advance moral and political goals through cooperation rather than coercion. Conventionally, the demand to be civil appears to be a simple, straightforward request asked of those with whom we come into contact, whether through in-person conversations or media communications. To achieve equality, we are exhorted to engage in behaviors that promote civility.

* This essay is based on remarks I delivered at an online panel, "Interrogating Civility," sponsored by the John Brademas Center of New York University, February 9, 2022, www.nyu.edu. I thank the organizers, Michael DiNiscia, Lynne Brown, Ellyn Toscano, and Ulrich Baer; and my fellow panelists, K. Anthony Appiah, Jonathan Haidt, and Catharine Stimpson. Devin Fergus, Jennifer M. Gülly, Nessa Rapoport, and Leslie Wingard provided many helpful suggestions.

Civility's Brutality

The term civility resonates with its popular, academic, and archaic meanings of politeness, citizenship, and civilization, respectively. It can also connote rational or reasoned discourse. The word is useful precisely because it is both ambiguous and expansive. But civility can also function under unequal conditions and as though unequal parties were equal ones. What happens when civility becomes its own end? Or when the accusation of incivility, whether directed toward the parties in disagreement or the source of the conflict, can itself be a means of foreclosing discussion and perpetuating further inequalities?

Accusations of incivility can and do often arise where unfairness and inequities are deeply entrenched, and civility can be used to pretend that parties agree, or that coercion is consent and compromise.[1] While many might think of civility as a hallmark of a fair and just society and believe that it facilitates and grants an equal voice to the dominant and marginalized alike, civility rarely helps balance the voices of the strong and weak, but is instead a weapon of the wealthy and powerful. When there are calls for civility, it is important to hold these advocates accountable for civility's uses that mask brutality and inequality.[2] Civility faces elite capture and co-optation, just as power, resources, and violence do.

A popular perception is that civility prevents violence through conduct and behaviors that might defuse aggressions and tensions, and then might lead instead to compromise, cooperation, or other prosocial behaviors. In fact, civility is about institutionalized power and violence. Yes, *civility,* which depends on power and violence to create and maintain it. Tavia Ngong'o and Kyla Wazana Tompkins identify how civility normalizes violence: "Civility discourse enforces a false equation between incivility and violence that works to mask everyday violence as a civic norm."[3] Violence is often posited as the extreme outcome of incivility. However, civility relies on violence as its counterpart.

More often attributed to *in*civility, power and violence establish and sustain the spaces cleared for those considered citizens in which their potential civility might flourish, where they can perform their civilized behaviors for each other. These civil spaces can be marked off by the physical buildings of polling sites and city council chambers where citizens can gather, and they can also extend to the geographic boundaries of national borders.[4] Or they can spread out through the international agreements that link US embassies and military bases abroad and such global bodies as the British Commonwealth, the G7, and the United Nations. Moreover, while present-day conversations about civility might assume local, political, or national communities, civility echoes beyond the nation-state, connecting territories that have been designated for "the First World"—European empires, Christendom, and White supremacy. Whether legally defined or imagined communities of like-minded people, cultures, and nations, these spaces for citizens share their inherent exclusions and are surrounded by spaces that are not civil.[5]

These civil spaces are heterogeneous as well, unevenly comprised of those who belong more and those who belong less. The silencing and slow deaths of elders, youths, immigrants, women, queer/trans+ people, disabled people, and people of color are just some of the ways in which the violence of civility is enacted in the public sphere.[6] In these additional contexts, people deemed rational and civilized by the powerful are thought to be the only ones fully capable of civility.[7]

The etymology of civility contains this exclusionary mechanism: the Latin word *civilitas* is based on *civilis*, "of or pertaining to citizens." Incivility, derived from *incivilitas,* is definitionally "not for citizens." This division may seem obvious on paper and in abstraction; however, divisions between citizens and noncitizens have been invoked to justify and trigger unrestrained, legally sanctioned brutalities—the worst of which are now considered crimes against humanity. Even if legal restrictions have been loosened over time, the descendants or perceived descendants of those who were once noncitizens continue to face the bigotry resulting from the incivility of their presumed illegitimate and undeserved citizenship.

The United States has its origins in exclusion: fewer than one-fourth of the adult population could vote in the early decades of the Republic, and lawmakers, local officials, and self-appointed law enforcers have repeatedly restricted the voting population through outright denial, intimidation, and terror.[8] Racist immigration and naturalization laws limited who could enter and reside in the United States and who could then become a citizen. Fundamentally, this nation is a settler colonial state, which was established and expanded through the violent erasure of Indigenous nations. The legacies of genocide and exclusion of Indigenous peoples continue to the present day. All these violent erasures affect the widespread perception of who is a citizen and who is not; who has "the right to have rights"; whose rights are protections that are carefully secured and defended and whose are not.[9] The repeated return of overt White supremacism to mainstream politics exposes that for a significant number of Americans, the conditions of restricted civility ought to be reestablished and violently reenforced as the law of the land.

Historically, civility also marked the behavior of citizens in contrast to that of soldiers.[10] A military protects the citizenry through violence or the threat of violence, and thus protects the corresponding places and spaces of civility. Invaders and settlers overemphasized the presence of native warriors or militaries in Africa and the Americas as the only political and social structures that existed, in contrast to the ostensibly more civilized governments and societies in Europe. This hierarchy of the civilized over the uncivilized and primitive justified imperialism and colonization. Like settler allies and their descendants today, European invaders refused to recognize the complex civil societies of non-European peoples as comparable to and rivaling their own. To the invaders, the putative lack of a civil society further indicated a lack of coeval civilizational development.[11] This alleged lack of civility was the spurious pretext for determining non-European peoples' incapacity for the necessary self- and societal discipline to sustain their own self-government.[12] The convenient evaluation of savagery and anti-Christian heathenism combined with the Hobbesian "state of nature" rationalized, illegitimately, European invasion, conquest, dispossession, and genocide.

There are other individual and institutional agents aside from the military that use violence to clear and maintain spaces for those not believed to be full citizens: for example, the criminal justice system, mass incarceration, border regimes, citizens' councils, nativist groups, and lynch mobs or other self-appointed law enforcers. Alongside cultivating civil spaces for citizens, nation-states develop and preserve spaces for noncitizens through reservations, prisons, immigrant detention centers, and refugee camps. These civil spaces are not always physically marked or permanent. They could be temporal and situational, depending on the time and people involved, such as sundown towns or public areas and facilities policed and prioritized for Whites. Exclusionary civil spaces also spring up in White/non-White interactions through de facto segregation in workplaces, neighborhoods, leisure activities, law enforcement, and surveillance on streets and highways—most notably, driving while Black and Brown. These kinds of civil spaces are delineated by whispers, gossip, maps, Confederate or White supremacist monuments, buildings, barbed wire, traffic barriers, policing, and the numbers of people who are regularly attacked or killed in these marked and unmarked borderlands.[13] Civility, in the name of so-called civilized society, on behalf of self-identified civilized people, in the continuance of US empire, does this.

Incivility is usually understood as a rupture of a perceived norm or past status quo: a rude comment or gesture, anger or raised voices that are surprising; groups of people gathering, marching, or occupying spaces that are not customarily used in these ways; or physical force or violence where none has occurred or been acknowledged before. Advocates of civility assume that civility has created or will create a level playing field among similarly situated parties to the debate. Politeness can be used to prove fairness and equality in a dialogue or negotiation. But given that all contractual discussions are coercive to some degree, participants are never similarly situated.[14] When there is civility, any party can plausibly contend that the conditions, processes, and outcomes are fair and equitable. But this logic fails to consider those cast out of civil spaces and violently barred from them. To perform civilized behaviors requires the exploitation, repression, or exclusion of the subordinated—who are, oftentimes, those people deemed uncivil. Civility creates a level playing field only through the so-called incivility of those who have never been allowed to play.

These exclusions may also be perpetuated in less visibly violent ways, through social hierarchies; forced assimilation; voter denial, suppression, or dilution; or the tacit threats or understood menace of Whites-only places and resources that are governmental institutions, neighborhoods, schools, or voting districts. Various peoples were legally designated noncitizens and uncivil; in addition to Indigenous and enslaved persons, non-White immigrants, specifically Asians, were kept out of the United States through immigration restrictions such as the 1882 Chinese Exclusion Act and 1917 Barred Zones Act. Those who were able to immigrate or were already living in the United States were excluded from the body politic as aliens ineligible for citizenship, a legal prohibition on naturalization that was upheld in the Supreme Court decisions *Takeo Ozawa* (1922) and *Bhagat Singh Thind* (1923).

Incivility is the historical norm. Civility is a paradoxical demand for people and communities to function as if they have not been denied full citizenship or accorded less importance in public debates when they are not silenced completely and treated as less than human. As a nation, we struggle with what is civil and uncivil, given this enduring history of violence over stolen land, labor, and freedom.

Playing Civility

With all these brutalities, exclusions, and inequities, why is civility still a useful concept, goal, or set of behaviors and practices? Why is incivility derided when it has proven an extremely effective strategy for sensational marketing, monetizing outrage, and motivating voters? Even within a citizenship status that confers the possibility of civility, there is a hierarchy: those with representation and influence in government above those on whose behalf the government supposedly acts. Amid competing interests, there are those whose rights are usually protected and whose voices are more likely to be heard. Elected officials are most responsive to Whites and donors—even those who are not their constituents.[15] In promoting civility, we can implicitly promote political and legal communities comprised of members with the right appearance, documents, and performances closely calibrated toward protecting White cis-heteropatriarchal norms. For example, despite workplace discrimination laws ostensibly protecting people who have been excluded from career advancement and equitable pay—women, BIPOC, disabled people—White cis-male employees are more likely to win their cases and to receive bigger average settlements for workplace discrimination than any other group.[16] Kept out of civil society for lengthier periods, Black defendants are prosecuted for more punitive sentences and have to wait longer for parole than Whites for similar crimes.[17] Being perceived as more civil means one is treated as more valuable—awarded more compensation for mistreatment, less punishment, and more freedom.

Demands for civility are usually top down, something to be extracted from those below. The powerful demand civility as a precondition to beginning negotiations, whereas those toward the bottom usually demand equality, dignity, and humanity rather than civility. Efforts toward civility by those at the top of the hierarchy are a way of managing the incivilities resulting from conflicts too long submerged or misidentified as the peaceful status quo. In negotiating the competing interests of nations, for example, international organizations such as the World Bank or the International Monetary Fund—dominated by wealthier US and European nations—force former European colonies into asymmetrical relationships; these alliances emphasize international cooperation while centering Global North priorities and profits. Or, on a much smaller scale, professional organizations may make limited opportunities available for some members from underrepresented groups, whom they select for their racial and gendered experiences rather than for career-building spotlights. In so doing, these organizations end up failing to advance and promote effective equity initiatives that address ongoing institutionalized harm from longstanding discrimination.

Oftentimes, the demand for a return to civility is a desire to return to a previous status quo. This demand comes from the strong as well as the weak; no matter what one's power over others and agency to change circumstances might be, attachments to and investments in civility are everywhere. Thus, a common strategy in moderating conflict is to delay, distract, and thwart addressing the issues sparking debate, such as demands for racial and gender equality. Instead, people invest their efforts in civility as the solution. They urge a return to the previous status quo to erase the conflicts at hand, even though those were the very conditions that gave rise to the tensions. Proponents of civility invent a previously harmonious time of peace and civility, overlooking how that peace and civility rested on the official and unofficial exclusion and silencing of dissent.

Whether in our workplaces, volunteer associations, or governments, leaders and representatives have a unique role and responsibility when they deploy these demands for civility. Their frequent strategy is to delay the engagement of members with different and dissenting ideas by encouraging them to wait to vote in another election cycle, or to hold off in applying or running for a leadership role. Essentially, if citizens or members do not abide by the codes of civility—generally interpreted to mean politely requesting or dutifully following procedures—then they don't get a voice or seat at the table. Or, more deceptively, they won't be determined to qualify for a seat nor deserve to be heard. BIPOC demands in particular are too often outside the bounds of "fair play," legitimate claims, or top priorities. Koritha Mitchell names the strategy of disciplining BIPOC demands as "know-your-place" aggression, a means of denying another's political voice as well as achievements: "How can we respect you when you don't know your place?"[18] Barbara Harris Combs posits "out of place" racism for Black and Brown voters.[19] The message is clear: go to the back, get in line, and wait for your name to be called or for conditions to change. When these dissenting citizens and members are finally allowed to vote, will their formerly excluded voices be heard with the same influence as others who have held their seats, voiced their opinions, and been listened to for years?

The irony, of course, is that current leaders and representatives are supposed to represent the interests of their constituencies, of which dissenting voices are a part. By representing only those they deem full citizens or members, leaders and organizations are engaging in civility through the de facto or de jure exclusion of more recent and less influential participants.

This exclusionary status quo persists even among attempts to correct racist practices and amid calls for civility. I analyze together two long-standing institutionalized harms that a major professional association of researchers and practitioners tried to address in recent years: the efforts of the American Psychological Association (APA) to reestablish the groundwork for civility in its professional organization; and official apologies from the APA for its role in perpetuating racism through psychology.[20] Other professional associations, such as the American Medical Association and the American Academy of Pediatrics, have tried to address their contribution to racism in medical research, health care practices, and public health advocacy. The APA followed with its own institutional self-evaluation of promoting racism in criminal justice, education, and health care since its founding in the 1850s.[21] Despite the APA's published apologies and anti-racist resolutions, critics exposed its lack of dialogue with the Association for Black Psychologists (ABPsi), Hispanic Psychological Association, Society of Indian Psychologists, Association of Asian American Psychologists, and other ethnic minority organizations whose criticisms have been ignored for decades.[22] The ABPsi responded to the APA's self-evaluation with its own letter, strongly questioning whether the same leadership and organization that have repeatedly promoted racist and discriminatory practices can fix their own institutional inequities without consulting the professional organizations formed by the critics, victims, and survivors of White supremacist psychological practices. That the APA officially believes it can do so extends its past racist exclusions of and harms to those left out of the APA's evaluative process, as well as limits the scope of its proposed redress, as the ABPsi leaders point out: "The American Psychological Association (APA) cannot simply dismiss the full history of Euro-American psychology that is rooted in a legacy of the pathology of Whiteness with a simple apology and questionable claims to now combat racism, oppression, and white hegemony. The APA, in fact, has played a large hand in the oppression of the Black community in education, health, housing, the media, the work sector, criminal justice, and practically all domains of life necessary to thriving and optimal well-being."[23]

This inadequate approach to institutional self-critique and inclusion is more visible in light of an earlier, intense debate within the APA membership that spurred demands for civility, recorded in the APA's journal on the profession in an article titled "Making APA Civil Again." To address the manner in which members conducted or behaved themselves in launching their arguments and criticisms, the APA created a working group on civility. The coauthors described the irony in the difficulties of their members trained in psychology to interact: "Although on the surface, one would expect that a large group of professional psychologists would be the last professional organization to have troubles with incivility given the nature of our profession and the principles expressed in our ethics code."[24] The working group created "operational definitions" for civility and incivility, a civility implementation plan, and suggested a civility ambassador for listservs and committees.[25]

The civility study arose from heated internal and public debates over the significant roles of APA leaders and members who used psychological methods and research to facilitate and supervise the torture of people through "enhanced" interrogation techniques held in "extraordinary rendition sites," such as Guantánamo Bay, in the US war on terror. In an open letter to the APA, leaders and allies of the American Middle Eastern North African Psychological Network criticized the APA's leadership that "colluded with U.S. governmental offices such as the Department of Defense (DOD), to the point of positioning our policies to align with those external bodies, thereby eroding our integrity as an independent organization, . . . and it is disgraceful that some in APA leadership ignored and dismissed the tireless voices of dissent and ethical consciousness along the way."[26]

Various dissenting groups were excluded from or silenced in the civil spaces the APA facilitated that promoted anti-Black racism or torture. The APA's efforts to increase civility are described in an article with a title "Making APA Civil Again" that echoes the "Make America Great Again" political slogan. Both these phrases prompt twinned questions about the extolled characteristics of American greatness and of APA civility, given the organization's advocating for or overlooking of racist brutalities, past and present. Pre-dating the war on terror, earlier eras of the APA's purported civility dovetail with its perpetuation of the systemic racism that it is arguably attempting to end and redress. For example, this putative *return* to civility has to obscure a little-acknowledged part of the Association's founding psychological research in the 19th century: how it served as a platform for its distinguished members to justify enslavement, genocide, and brutal punishments with pseudoscientific psychological theories.[27] If the APA, other professional organizations, or US mainstream politics were ever civil in a supposedly benign past to which we are encouraged to return, who and what injustices will continue to be ignored, silenced, or excluded for this previous civility to reign again? It is impossible to make the APA civil *again* and make America *civil* again if they never were.

Civility's Ends

Civility is both deceptively expansive and restrictive. It is expansive in that its archaic definitions still resonate today and have a legacy of systemic brutality that has never been fully redressed or reckoned with, if at all. It is restrictive in that only some people are considered civil, capable of or deserving of others' civility.

By overestimating civility's impact, whether optimistically or deceptively, leaders and policymakers invest time, resources, and energy into calling for and relying on civility to make people feel heard and thereby manage inequalities. Instead of cultivating other principles that can be used to describe civility, such as mutual respect, reciprocity, accountability, or responsibility, civility is much too often merely a rallying cry, likely because of its deeply rooted connection to citizenship: what citizens owe to each other, what citizens owe to the state. Or, perhaps more accurately, which behaviors citizens owe to each other, and which behaviors citizens owe to the state. Institutional leaders manage conflicts in unproductive ways, oftentimes at the expense of addressing the conditions that give rise to the conflicts themselves.

While I recognize the greater agency of institutional leaders to demand civility, I am also advocating a marshaling of whatever collective power those less powerful members, workers, participants, and voters might have, as well as those who think they are bystanders to these conflicts. The public of public opinion must continue to expose these delay-and-distract strategies that return negotiations to a historically elite concept of citizenship and the further silencing of the have-nots who are forced to prove daily and in every interaction that they are civil beings worthy of equality, humanity, and dignity.

Civility isn't the pat solution it is made out to be. Too ambiguous and open-ended, lack of civility is a highly suspect diagnosis.

We should be especially skeptical of and reject demands for civility that are deployed to quell dissent by marginalized populations and that dampen a democratic future.

NOTES

1 For a fuller discussion of how the famed legislative compromises of the antebellum era were agreements among elite White male interests overriding the interests of dispossessed Indigenous and enslaved African peoples, see Lynn Mie Itagaki, "Compromising Trust," *Missouri Law Review* 86, no. 2 (2021): 541–52.

2 For an overview of the "civility debates" connected to multiculturalism and the aftermath of the Cold War, see Lynn Mie Itagaki, *Civil Racism: The 1992 Los Angeles Rebellion and the Crisis of Racial Burnout* (University of Minnesota Press, 2016), 6–23.

3 Tavia Nyong'o and Kyla Wazana Tompkins, "Eleven Theses on Civility," *Social Text Online* (July 11, 2018), socialtextjournal.org.

4 Elsewhere, I have discussed these civil spaces in terms of the workplace and websites for discriminations that LGBTQ+ workers and users with disabilities have faced: Lynn Mie Itagaki, "The Long Con of Civility," special issue, "How We Argue Now: The Moral Foundations of Politics and Law," *Connecticut Law Review* 52, no. 3 (February 2021): 1183–85.

5 I deliberately use the adjective "civil" over "civic" spaces, despite *civic*'s same Latinate root definition in "citizen" or *civis*. Although "civic" and "civil" can be synonyms, I posit that "civic" has a more restricted use and range of connotations, whereas "civil(ity)" is more expansive, as discussed above.

In my reference to "noncitizens," Indigenous peoples within US borders were not specifically recognized as US citizen-voters until the Snyder Act of 1924, and states were still allowed to deny them the franchise. As another example, in World War II, US-born citizens of Japanese descent were stripped of their birthright citizenship and reclassified as 4-C enemy "aliens," a term reserved for immigrants, during their imprisonment in Japanese American incarceration camps.

6 See Lauren Berlant, "Slow Death (Sovereignty, Obesity, Lateral Agency)," *Critical Inquiry* 33, no. 4 (Summer 2007): 754–80.

7 In Spanish colonialism, the *gente de razón*, these so-called people of reason, were those Indigenous peoples who did not resist invasion and

colonization and largely assimilated into European culture. I thank Victor Goldgel-Caballo for this insight.

8 Dave Umhoefer, "Mark Pocan Says Less than 25 Percent of Population Could Vote When Constitution Was Written," Politifact, April 16, 2015, www.politifact.com.

9 Hannah Arendt, *The Origins of Totalitarianism* (Harcourt Brace Jovanovich, 1976), 296–98.

10 Thy Phu, *Picturing Model Citizens: Civility in Asian American Visual Culture* (Temple University Press, 2011), 5.

11 See Johannes Fabian, *Time and the Other: How Anthropology Makes Its Object* (Columbia University Press, 1983).

12 Citing Thomas Hobbes's *Leviathan* and John Locke's *Second Treatise on Government,* Robert Nichols explains how Europeans' illegitimate and immoral dispossessions of land were made legitimate and moral: "Historically, the philosophical and legal traditions of European societies and their settler-colonies have not merely understood indigenous peoples to lack land entitlement. Rather, they failed to accept that indigenous peoples had sufficiently civilized forms of social and political association to possess a form of rule or imperium that needed to be respected at all. Hobbes claimed, for instance, that the peoples of the America 'have no government at all' and Locke and Grotius, while recognizing indigenous peoples had some form of political association, concluded that this rule was little more than that of generals over armies, and, thus, they could be said to exercise only 'a very moderate sovereignty'"; see "Indigeneity and the Settler Contract Today," *Philosophy and Social Criticism* 39, no. 2 (2013): 175.

13 I allude here to Gloria Anzaldúa's landmark *Borderlands/La Frontera: The New Mestiza* (Aunt Lute, 1984), and the fields of study such as border studies and women of color feminism that are indebted to her thinking.

14 In her book-length collaboration with Charles Mills, Carole Pateman identifies the coercion involved in any social contract. Patemen's position that coercion is always present differs from Mills's belief that contract theory could equalize parties engaged in the social contract; see *Contract and Domination* (Polity, 2007), 17. For a fuller discussion of this important difference between Pateman and Mills in the coercive impact of these differential power relations between and among contractual parties in the persistent violences of the settler colonial state, see Nichols, "Indigeneity and the Settler Contract Today," 165–86.

15 David Callahan and J. Mijin Cha, "Stacked Deck: How the Dominance of Politics by the Affluent & Business Undermines Economic Mobility in America," Dēmos, February 2013, www.demos.org.

16 In her reevaluation of intersectionality, Anna Carastathis identifies the concept's limited impact on employment discrimination for Black women specifically and BIPOC generally: "If the failure of US courts to redress discrimination against Black women by corporate employers is surprising, how can we reconcile the fact that white male plaintiffs, in whose favor courts have an existing presumption, more easily and more profitably win suits charging employment discrimination than do women and men of color and white women?" "Basements and Intersections," *Hypatia* 28, no. 4 (Fall 2013): 701; Rachel Kahn Best, Linda Hamilton Krieger, Lauren B. Edelman, and Scott R. Eliason note that "plaintiffs who make intersectional claims are only half as likely to win their cases as plaintiffs who allege a single basis of discrimination," in "Multiple Disadvantages: An Empirical Test of Intersectionality Theory in EEO Litigation," Stanford Sociology of Law Workshop, March 3, 2011.

17 Inter-American Commission on Human Rights, "Police Violence Against Afro-descendants in the United States," (2018), www.oas.org; United Nations Human Rights Office, "Promotion and Protection of the Human Rights and Fundamental Freedoms of Africans and of People of African Descent Against Excessive Use of Force and Other Human Rights Violations by Law Enforcement Officers," June 28, 2021, 9, www.ohchr.org.

18 Koritha Mitchell, "Identifying White Mediocrity and Know-Your-Place Aggression: A Form of Self-Care," *African American Review* 51, no. 4 (Winter 2018): 259.

19 See Barbara Harris Combs, "Black (and Brown) Bodies Out of Place: Towards a Theoretical Understanding of Systematic Voter Suppression in the United States," *Critical Sociology* 42, nos. 4–5 (2016): 535–49.

20 Thomas G. Plante, "Making APA Civil Again: The Efforts and Outcomes of the Civility Working Group," *Professional Psychology: Research and Practice* 48, no. 6 (2017): 401–2.

21 The APA timeline aggregated "examples of harm that we and other historians have deemed most salient and impactful based on our assessment of the extent to which they serve as exemplars of repeated and prominent trends in the field's history and their degree of direct connection with organized psychology"; see "Historical Chronology," 2021, www.apa.org.

22 See Evan Auguste, Wade Nobles, and Daryl Rowe, "Why the APA's Apology for Promoting White Supremacy Falls Short," NBC News, November 21, 2021, www.nbcnews.com; and "APA's Commitment to Addressing Systemic Racism," APA, 2021, www.apa.org.

23 "ABPsi's Full Statement," ABPSI, November 24, 2021, https://abpsi.org, 1.

24 Plante, "Making APA Civil Again," 401.

25 Plante, 402–3.

26 American MENA Psychological Network et al., "Open Letter to the American Psychological Association & the Psychological Community by the American Middle Eastern/North African (MENA) Psychological Network," APA, August 14, 2015, www.apa.org.

27 "ABPsi's Full Statement," 2.

4

Notes Toward a New Decorum

CATHARINE R. STIMPSON

Why do people praise civility? And people who are civil?[1]

Unfortunately, as an ideal and social practice, civility carries a lot of baggage. Historically, it defined the active citizen—when active citizenship might be limited to one class, gender, or race. Moreover, civility has defined the cultured person—when ideas of culture might be limited to one nation, race, or group. Finally, civility has defined the polite person, the well-mannered person—when politesse and good manners might be the deceptive public performance of someone who is impolite, badly mannered, even brutal and hypocritical in private.

Despite this heavy baggage, our society needs civility in order to sustain itself. Why is this so? It is so simply because nearly all of us are as capable of dealing out pain as we are of bestowing love—in our private or public lives. Homo sapiens has been cruelly intelligent in building vast portfolios of ways to administer physical or psychological suffering, or both. The internet is but our latest investment in how to deal out psychological suffering.

We can starve people, or deprive them of psychological sustenance, or inflict bullying, beatings, batterings, and torture—or do all of these at once. Having power fails to guarantee the refusal to do harm. On the contrary, having power too often enables the capacity for doing harm. Power is a permission slip for hurting others. This is true of public authorities, undisciplined troops, gangs, a rapist seizing power, or a sadist who believes he or she can torment another with impunity. Sadists want their victim to feel pain and to acknowledge the sadist's ability to inflict it, but they can often hide, in cowardly ways, from anyone seeing it.

One of the most desperately serious of questions is how we can reduce, mitigate, remediate, or police harm. One answer focuses on governments. They can have laws that criminalize such horrors. To focus on psychological pain alone, in American law, courts can convict someone for causing "pain and suffering," or "intentional infliction of emotional distress," or "mental anguish," or "negligent infliction of emotional distress." Fortunately, some members of the legal community are also newly aware that legal processes must also protect victims from being retraumatized during them.

However, if good enough governments are necessary, they are not sufficient. This is so for at least two reasons. First, governments themselves can do harm, grievous harm—even good enough democratic governments. Next, even with some laws on the books, psychological harms can be hidden, invisible, and inaudible to all but the closest of observers. Painfully, such harms occur with rape victims. The need to veil pain is one feature of the aftermath of the crime itself.

The democratic state that seeks to heal as well as to police psychological harms must investigate these hidden harms with care and wisdom. To help men and boys, the state (and its agents) must realize that under the strictures of toxic manhood, men and boys can shut up and "suck up" their pain, surely an awful metaphor. However, toxic manhood has another, more overt side. Men and boys can spew misogynistic insults and then shrug them away as "freedom of speech" or "comedy."[2] Do not misunderstand me. I love comedy. Some comedians can seem uncivil, but they are our truth-tellers. However, misogynistic men and boys lack both civility and comedic talent. They are simply mouthing off.

To help women and girls, the state (and its agents) must also realize that under the strictures of toxic womanhood, women and girls are fearful—and often with good reason. Those who speak out about both physical and psychological harms, acts of self-witnessing, may be silenced, disbelieved, ridiculed, or punished. To cry out, "I am in danger," can be an invitation to ostracism or further violence.

To help trans and nonbinary people, the state can recognize the richness of their identities and, when they are adults, their full citizenship. They are neither freaks nor handy scapegoats for a society eager for freaks to scapegoat.

Now, let us hopefully assume that civility can rid itself of its historical baggage. As hopefully, let us further assume that civility can be inclusive rather than exclusive. If these assumptions can become a part of everyday life, civility can play a crucial political and social role. *In active parallel processing with laws, civility can offer a set of norms for political and social relations that reject the infliction of suffering. If enough people behave in accord with these norms, more caring and lively communities will emerge.*

But now let us imagine the substance of what a new set of norms might be. I have thought up such a set and called it the New Decorum.[3] I prefer the term "decorum" to "civility" because decorum signifies appropriate behaviors across all social and political zones, while civility seems more rooted in the civil and the political. However, I can understand why people, reading this essay, might easily rename my New Decorum the New Civility. Adherence to the name matters far less than adherence to the behaviors that the name signifies. Do what you want with the name. Do what you must to stop suffering.

The Old Decorum carries with it some of the same baggage as the concept of civility. When civility is prized, men are more apt to model and perform it. Some roots of this masculinization of civility are no doubt in that association of civility with "civil" and the public sphere. When decorum is prized, women are more apt to model and perform it. Some roots of this feminization of decorum are arguably in the Latin *decorum,* which can mean propriety, grace, beauty. Because gender codes are inseparable from power structures, a decorous woman has learned to be subordinate and submissive to the men of her class—the judges, pastors, fathers, brothers, and, often, sons.

However, these decorous women have their own powers. White decorous women, even at a disadvantage in subordination to men, have powers that women of color do not. As Rafia Zakaria writes succinctly and with some understatement, "The assumption that women of color and white women all stand at the same disadvantage is flawed."[4]

The New Decorum has three imperatives, First, scour, scrape away at, and dump the historical baggage of the Old Decorum. Second, stop inflicting unwarranted suffering.[5] Follow the familiar injunction "Do no harm." The words we associate with medical education should be a commandment to us all. If one is harmed, one must have the ability to speak about it and be heard. The third imperative is a deep consideration of others, for their selfhood and bodily autonomy. This necessarily demands some personal restraint. The "I" must often check its self-perceived needs in the presence of "The Other"—for example, the need to fondle or kiss a subordinate, or make a stupid misogynistic crack, or be a bully in order to show a skeptical audience that you have muscle.

These three imperatives of the New Decorum—get rid of the baggage of the Old, do no harm, deeply consider others—would spring into action in many situations. One, in contemporary America, is the lives of trans children and people. Our norms would prohibit sneers, insults, the denial of appropriate medical procedures, and violence against trans children and people. Our norms would respect their claiming of their own sexual and gender identity. Let the child courteously, mindfully use the damned bathroom of his/her/their choice.[6]

A reality of the New Decorum is that the giving and earning of respect is hard, endless work. As Richard Sennett has observed, "Respect is an expressive performance. That is, treating others with respect doesn't just happen, even with the best will in the world; to convey respect means finding the words and gestures which make it felt and convincing."[7] To be respectful demands recognizing the human capacity for inflicting harm, as well as the vast range of differences among us and the potentially harmful power relations they inevitably embody. Then, after the recognition of differences, each of us must ask, "What are the differences that I fear? Or that I disdain? Or that I find intolerable? Or that I must crush and control?" Answering these questions demands self- and social interrogation. These questions are a necessary beginning to changes in behavior.

The New Decorum is not a recipe for mealy-mouthed speech. On the contrary, it celebrates freedom of speech, thought, and of the arts.

The New Decorum is not an etiquette lesson in sweet insincerities. On the contrary, it relies on a sincerity that refuses the temptations of meanness and malice. Significantly, the New Decorum is not a demand for the repression of righteous anger about the infliction of harm. On the contrary, nonviolence social and political movements—in their language and activities—can be paradigms of the New Decorum in sweeping public action.

Let me offer two, more focused, perhaps surprising examples of the language of the New Decorum in the public arena.

They are speeches that demand the cessation of harm, but, in their rhetoric and demeanor in the presentation of their demands, they are case studies of how the New Decorum can operate.[8] My first example is a legendary performance in American history, "Ain't I a Woman?" by Sojourner Truth. She delivered this speech at a convention in Ohio in October 1851. We have two versions of it. One was published in an antislavery paper a month after she spoke. The famous interrogative, "Ain't I a Woman," is not there. The second version was published, with a women's rights editor, in 1863. This is the text we have. In brief, we are in the presence of some textual indeterminacy, but the two versions are substantially the same.

The date 1851 is significant. Only 24 years before, the State of New York had abolished slavery within its borders—on July 4, 1827. In 12 years, on January 1, 1863, Abraham Lincoln would issue the Emancipation Proclamation, abolishing slavery in rebel-held territory. Sojourner Truth is bearing witness to the profound evil and sin of slavery.

Sojourner Truth had been born into slavery in 1797 in New York. Her slave name was Isabella Baumfree. Her master and mistress were harsh and abusive. In 1826, she had been promised her freedom, a promise her master then broke. Taking an infant daughter, but forced to leave her other children behind, she escaped to freedom. Later, she would go to court to gain the freedom of one of her sons, sold into slavery in Alabama. She won—an extraordinary event. She was a religious visionary and an Evangelical preacher of great conviction. She took the name Sojourner Truth in 1843.

The symbolism of the name is vivid. She is temporarily here on earth. While she is on such a journey, she will tell of truths of heaven and earth. She will become an abolitionist, a believer in women's rights (with caveats), an author, and an activist. Her faith united these convictions. She was to die in 1883, a bitter time in the United States, as white supremacy began to take hold anew after the end of post-Civil War Reconstruction.

As a teacher and preacher, Sojourner Truth uses her own body as her syllabus. Her flesh and blood are her curriculum. So doing, she is proudly courageous. She calls out members of her audience, who may be her social and racial "superiors," but they are her students. She dares them to hear her truths. However, she is also clever and sly. She first presents herself as that familiar and reassuring figure, a mother. Then, in direct and colloquial speech, she—this Black woman, once a suffering slave—presents herself as "a woman." She is no beast of burden, but a woman. Radical though this is, she goes on to claim that she has a mind, a brain. She is a thinking woman, even if she may not know the word "intellect." That is one of her sly touches. Then, she reminds her audience that she, like all women, represents the pathway between heaven and earth. Abused though her womb has been by her master, she is a symbol of the birth of Jesus. After these radical teachings about the magnitude of a Black woman, she ends courteously, politely—as a woman conventionally should. She thanks her audience, and tells them that she has nothing more to say. Now, it is the turn of her audience to practice what I call the New Decorum; but, made rugged and radiant by Truth's visions, the New Decorum becomes synonymous with virtue. Its practitioners transvalue traditional "decorum" into a quest for ethical practices that can and must supplement and invigorate the law.

My second example is many decades later, a speech by Alexandria Ocasio-Cortez, known familiarly as AOC. Obviously, the United States has changed, but harms remain. Ocasio-Cortez is one of the most charismatic of younger politicians in the United States. She was born in 1989 in the Bronx, the poorest borough in New York City. She was educated there, until her father was able to move his family to the suburbs, where she attended high school. However, she continued to visit her extended family in the Bronx. She studied economics and international relations at Boston University, graduating in 2011. She worked in the office of the late Senator Edward "Ted" Kennedy, and then helped to organize Latinx youth in the Bronx and nationally. To support her family after her father's death, she was a waitress and a barista—those women's jobs. In 2016, she volunteered for Bernie Sanders in his US presidential campaign. Then, in 2018, after tireless organizing, she defeated a powerful congressman—White, male, older, comparatively liberal—and entered Congress. Her causes were racial justice, environmental justice, and economic justice. She gained national publicity because of her electoral upset, but also because she is so smart, funny, articulate, and fearless.

AOC's speech about sexual harassment in Congress, made on July 23, 2020, has become legendary. She has taken the floor of the US House of Representatives. She never rants; she never sneers. Her own language and demeanor are appropriate to the dignity of this setting. As she will remind us, she belongs here. She is a congresswoman, with constituents who elected her and whom she will serve. She is the "gentlewoman from New York." Other legislators are standing with her.

Her speech begins with a personal story in which another congressman—Ted Yoho—has demeaned her crudely and rudely. He has ended with the hostile vulgarity of "fucking bitch." Yoho's language is familiar to her—from her jobs, from the streets. Indeed, that familiarity is part of the shock of the story. She was tempted to ignore him, but Yoho added insult to injury. He gave a faux apology to the House, arguing that because he has a wife and daughters, he could not be a misogynist.

Then, AOC felt she must speak—for herself and for other women. She cannot permit younger women—for example, her nieces—to believe a Yoho is acceptable. She cannot permit her mother to believe that she will ignore the lesson her mother and her father taught her: never accept abuse. Clearly, efficiently, and devastatingly, AOC expands her story from that of her own experience to a far more general exposure of male power and privilege. It shows a "pattern" of dehumanization. It gives men permission to abuse women. Disgustingly, men—like Congressman Yoho—hide behind their wives and daughters. Such men claim they must be good "about women," because they have wives and daughters. At best, these men confuse correlation and causation.

But, AOC says, I am a daughter, too. I am younger than Congressman Yoho's younger daughter. If you, Congressman Yoho, abuse me, you are enabling other men to abuse them. "Decent" men treat everyone decently, not just their wives and daughters. Congressman Yoho has now become AOC's student. Then, like Sojourner Truth, in a gracious act stripped of any obsequiousness, she thanks the congressman for teaching her how power works, how accosting women works.

I have no confidence that Congressman Yoho is capable of learning from AOC. However, a multitude of citizens were.

A reconstituted civility, or my New Decorum, would be messy and slow to become a social and cultural reality. The powerful would no doubt do what the powerful so often do, cling to their balconies and their guns and warplanes and control of disinformation. In easy circumstances, the New Decorum would entail good sense, amiability, a grasp of truth, interwoven with kindness and courage. In harsher circumstances, the New Decorum would embody and emblazon virtues that women have exercised historically and today. Rafia Zakaria writes of some of them: "Growing up in Pakistan, I saw my mother, my grandmother, and my aunts survive terrible suffering of all sorts. They survived migrations, devastating business losses, inept husbands, lost relations, legal discrimination, and so much more, without ever giving in to despair, without ever abandoning those who relied on them, without ever failing to show up. Their resilience, their sense of responsibility, their empathy, and their capacity for hope are also feminist qualities."[9]

The New Decorum, or, if you prefer, the New Civility, is at heart a call for the dissolution of the cruelties of our species, which run the gamut from loutish stupidities to the application of sophisticated braininess, and for the growth of a virtuous wisdom—before it is too late.

NOTES

1 I had drafted sections of this paper before Russia wrongly and cruelly invaded Ukraine. I edited sections on June 25, 2022, the day after the Supreme Court of the United States issued its wrong and cruel decision about *Roe v. Wade*. They are very different actions, one a major display of military force that revels in its brutal destructiveness; the other a display of legal force that self-righteously proclaims the righteousness of its own destructiveness. However, both are exercises of power that make my recommendations for a civil society at once necessary and Utopian.

2 I realize that we can have both misogynistic and misanthropic comic diatribes, satires, and irony. The boundary between them lies in the incitement of violence where there is no framing device such as a classroom, a critical reading, or a community of readers/auditors to drain that violence of its contagion.

3 I introduced this concept in my paper "Dereliction, Due Process, and Decorum: The Crises of Title IX," *Signs: Journal of Women in Culture and Society* 47, no. 2 (Winter 2022): 261–93.

4 Rafia Zakaria, *Against White Feminism* (W. W. Norton, 2021), 10.

5 What might warranted suffering be? Some examples: 1) the pain of childbirth; 2) the pain of recovering from a major accident or surgery; 3) the pain of creating a work of art or performance; 4) the grief at the loss of a beloved one. (Even these can be ameliorated or exacerbated, at times considerably.)

6 In 2022, the State of Texas began its legal efforts to criminalize medical treatments for trans youth as child abuse.

7 Richard Sennett, *Respect in a World of Inequality* (W. W. Norton 2003), 207.

8 I first discussed these texts at a "Conference on Feminist Pedagogies," Ca' Foscari University, Venice, September 10, 2020.

9 Zakaria, *Against White Feminism*, 10–11. Significantly, Zakaria continues that the "current feminist arithmetic will [not] permit" these qualities. "In the value system of white feminism, it is rebellion, rather than resilience, that is seen as the ultimate feminist virtue." I have learned a lot from Zakaria, but would argue that feminist virtues often include resilience.

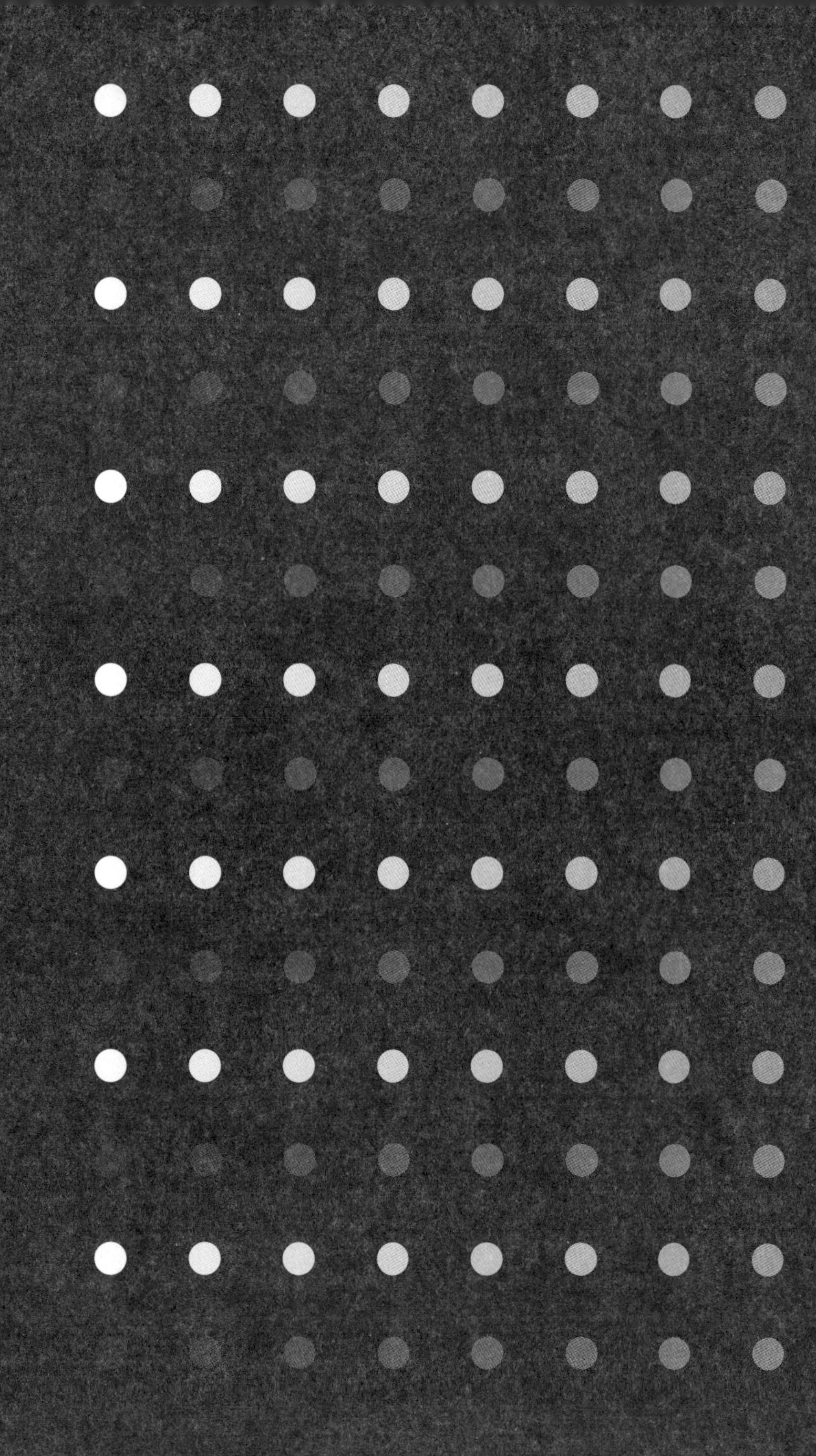

PART II

Politics, Political Institutions, and Democracy

5

Tribal Politics

The Breakdown of Norms and the Crisis of Civility

NORMAN J. ORNSTEIN

Incivility is not a new phenomenon in American politics. As Julia Azari points out, the history of the United States is that we've had long periods when civility was not a common theme.[1]

Harsh language and wild charges in political campaigns go back to the beginning of the Republic. The 1800 presidential campaign was one that the National Constitution Center said "rivals any current presidential campaign for insults and rancor."[2] In that campaign, Thomas Jefferson's hired hand, James Callender, published an attack on Adams that described him as "a hideous hermaphroditical character which has neither the force and firmness of a man, not the gentleness and sensibility of a woman."

In her book *Field of Blood*, the great Yale historian Joanne Freeman makes it powerfully clear that violence was a not-infrequent response to political differences in eras past.[3] There were, after all, duels before the Civil War. Times weren't exactly civil in 1856, when South Carolina representative Preston Brooks went over to the Senate and, with his cane, beat abolitionist senator Charles Sumner of Massachusetts senseless, putting him out of commission for years.

At the same time, if we fast forward to the twentieth century, President Franklin Delano Roosevelt said, in a notable speech in 1936, "We had to struggle with the old enemies of peace—business and financial monopoly, speculation, reckless banking, class antagonism, sectionalism, war profiteering. They had begun to consider the Government of the United States as a mere appendage to their own affairs. We know now that Government by organized money is just as dangerous as Government by organized mob. Never before in all our history have these forces been so united against one candidate as they stand today. They are unanimous in their hate for me—and I welcome their hatred."[4]

In 1964, South Carolina senator Strom Thurmond wrestled outside a committee room with his colleague Texas senator Ralph Yarborough. In 1985, New York Democratic representative Tom Downey was grabbed by the throat by Republican Bob Dornan of California after Dornan had called him a "wimp," a scene called by the *Washington Post* "Duel on the Hill."[5]

If history gives us vivid examples of outrageous rhetoric and violence, today's discourse is, on one level, par for the course. But, for many reasons, it is not business as usual, or something to be trivialized or downplayed.

When I first came to Washington, in the fall of 1969, the speaker of the House was John McCormick. John McCormick was famous for never using epithets. When I used to teach about Congress, I would say that when McCormick got particularly upset with an opponent, he went on the floor and said, "I hold the distinguished gentleman in minimum high regard."

That's what passed for his epithets then. Five decades ago, norms were strong.

In 1960, in a seminal book called *U.S. Senators and Their World*, Donald R. Matthews wrote about the Senate's folkways. Among them was courtesy:

> A cardinal rule of Senate behavior is that political disagreements should not influence personal feelings. . . . Few opportunities to praise publicly a colleague are missed in the Senate. . . . This kind of behavior—avoiding personal attacks on colleagues, striving for impersonality by divorcing the self from the office, "buttering up" the opposition by extending unsolicited compliments—is thought by the senators to pay off in legislative results. Personal attacks, unnecessary unpleasantness, and pursuing a line of thought or action that might embarrass a colleague needlessly are all thought to be self-defeating. "After all, your enemies on one issue may be your friends on the next." Similar considerations also suggest the undesirability of excessive partisanship. . . . They also suggest, despite partisan differences, that one senator should hesitate to campaign against another.[6]

Of course, civility can also legitimize illegitimate or wrongful behavior, as was true for decades in the Senate over segregation. It has also been true recently within the Supreme Court, where justices trying to preserve the court's reputation for judiciousness fail to call out decisions that are partisan or ideological in nature.

In 2004, when Senate Republican leader Bill Frist campaigned in South Dakota against his Democratic counterpart, Tom Daschle, the campaign signaled the demise of one part of that folkway; Lindsey Graham's angry rant against his Democratic colleagues on the Judiciary Committee during the Supreme Court confirmation hearings for Brett Kavanaugh signaled the demise of the rest.

During his tenure in the House, Mickey Edwards experienced a time when the norms were strong, reinforced by leaders like Tip O'Neill and Bob Michel. But Edwards was also present at the catalyst of the changes that led to our current corrosive tribalism. Of course, one component of this change was the larger and broader change in the regional alignment of our politics, dating back at least to the 1960s, as the South moved from the stronghold of the Democratic Party to that of the Republicans, while New England and the Pacific West went from bastions of liberal and moderate Republicans to firmly blue regions. Parties that had been mixtures of liberals and conservatives gradually became more homogeneous and more divided ideologically—what we now call "polarization."

But polarization does not automatically bring incivility, an unwillingness to compromise or to follow the regular order of legislative policymaking. Enter Republican Newt Gingrich, speaker of the House, who consciously moved to blow up norms and to create the tribal era in which we live. Newt's goal, to end the Democrats' hegemony in the House, was articulated as soon as he arrived as a freshman in 1979. At a series of dinners Tom Mann and I arranged at the American Enterprise Institute (AEI) with several freshmen from the Class of 1978, Gingrich outlined his strategy and tactics to break a stranglehold on the majority Democrats had held for 24 consecutive years.

Gingrich believed that he had to destroy the advantages incumbents had in separating themselves from broader political trends, an edge greater for members of the majority. To do so meant changing the narrative and making Congress look so awful to voters that they would finally opt for a change, throwing the ins out and bringing the outs in. That, in turn, meant radicalizing his own party, provoking the majority to overreact, playing on the eagerness of the press to cover conflict and controversy, and effectively tribalizing politics. He used the ethics process to criminalize policy differences—as he did with his charge against Speaker Jim Wright, leading to his downfall—and got his members and candidates to focus on language.

Here are some of the terms, crafted in conjunction with Frank Luntz, that Gingrich taught Republicans in 1990 to apply to Democrats: anti-child, anti-flag, betray, bizarre, cheat, corruption, crisis, decay, destroy, devour, disgrace, excuses, greed, hypocrisy, incompetent, liberal, machine, obsolete, pathetic, radical, red tape, self-serving, sensationalists, sick, status quo, steal, traitors, welfare.[7]

He accomplished his goal, of course, in 1994. In the decades since, the tribal divisions metastasized to the states and to voters. What tribalization did was to create a different mindset and frame for lawmakers and voters alike. Instead of viewing those in the other party as adversaries—worthy Americans who are simply misguided—opponents were now seen as evil people trying to destroy our way of life. Gingrich recruited candidates who reflected those views, including virulent anti-government and anti-institutional sentiments. Norms and rules no longer mattered. Some of those candidates moved to the Senate, where they inculcated the same values into that body, reflected well in Sean Theriault's book *The Gingrich Senators.*[8]

At the same time that Gingrich was moving us in that direction, he was getting help from the expansion of tribal media, which was triggered in 1987–88 by the Federal Communications Commission's vote to end the Fairness Doctrine and the subsequent advent of social media. That change in communications chipped away at the fundamental norms of discourse and civility in society as a whole and reinforced their decline in Congress and elsewhere. All of us who are using social media know that people sometimes, behind the cloak of anonymity, will say outrageous and awful, racist, anti-Semitic, and other hateful things. And now, many no longer even care enough to hide behind anonymity.

After Gingrich, the next consequential series of events followed the financial collapse in 2008. The desperate move to keep the catastrophe limited—led by President George W. Bush and his treasury secretary, Hank Paulson, joined by all congressional leaders of both parties—was first rejected by House Republicans before a sharp stock market drop brought enough of them along to pass a bailout package. But the dynamic resulted in a Tea Party movement that itself led to right-wing populism, characterized by disdain among Republican candidates for all elites, as well as isolationism, protectionism, and anti-immigrant nativism. These attitudes persisted well after the economy recovered. Leaders who encouraged and responded to the anti-government, populist appeals, including "Young Guns" Kevin McCarthy, Paul Ryan, and Eric Cantor, achieved political success with the 2010 midterm campaign and its historic gains in the House, but also helped shape a party that in 2012 Tom Mann and I characterized this way: "The Republican Party has become an insurgent outlier—ideologically extreme; contemptuous of the inherited social and economic policy regime; scornful of compromise; unpersuaded by conventional understanding of facts, evidence and science; and dismissive of the legitimacy of its political opposition."[9]

All of this preceded the emergence of Donald Trump as candidate and president, but he became a massive accelerant of what Gingrich started. When you call a judge "a Mexican judge," refer to your opponents during the campaign as "little Marco" and "lyin' Ted," accuse a candidate—Ted Cruz, as Trump did—of having his father participate in the plot to assassinate JFK, you establish a prevailing tone, with contemptuous and contemptible language and with calls to violence repeated during rallies, not just during the campaign but throughout Trump's presidency, including in the lead-up to the violent insurrection at the Capitol on January 6. The fact that Republicans effectively legitimized and protected Trump in its aftermath, refusing to convict him after impeachment and filibustering an effort to create a bipartisan commission to get to the bottom of the seditious activity, does not augur well.

The president is the big opinion leader. The way Trump shaped views and fostered divisions was set at his Inauguration, a bombastic speech in which he referred to "American carnage." Of course, he is not the only president, nor are Republicans the only party who have used provocative rhetoric; Julia Azari may be right that a couple of things Barack Obama said shook the fabric a bit. But the juxtaposition is like comparing jaywalking to felony assault.

If you look at our political life through a lens of tribalism, where you see people on the other side of the aisle not as worthy Americans but as enemies, and if you as president refer to violent white supremacists in Charlottesville as "very fine people," you are setting the stage for very bad outcomes. Surveys reflect this state of affairs, including one conducted by my institution, AEI, in its monthly Community Survey—one of the finest—that shows 30 percent of Republicans, and barely a trace element of Democrats, believe that violence is appropriate if people are trying to chip away at or destroy your way of life.[10]

And now, with social media, including the way in which malign foreign actors and domestic ones are spreading lies and using these platforms with, I would say, the active cognizance of Facebook and others to divide people and inflame judgments, we find ourselves in an extremely difficult place.

When you have members of Congress who, for example, speak at white supremacist rallies, as Paul Gosar and Marjorie Taylor Greene did, and their own party leader refuses either to condemn them or take action against them, it tells us that we're on a sadly downward slope towards a much more difficult political system than we've had. As my friend and mentor the late Daniel Patrick Moynihan said: You define deviancy down. What used to be absolutely shocking years ago has become commonplace and normal now.

I'm hoping that an expansion of the practice of debate in schools and elsewhere, where participants learn to inhabit and argue opposing positions and viewpoints, might help a little bit at the grassroots level. But until there is some way of holding people accountable with shame, at least, for violating essential norms of behavior, we're not going to get out of the mess we're in. And we're not going to find it easy, not only to make policy that benefits the country as a whole, or to deal with issues that threaten our national security, but to keep from a shattering of the fundamentals that cement and hold our society together.

We face an existential threat to our constitutional system. Our predicament is worse than what we've seen in our lifetimes, and it's not going to get better anytime soon.

NOTES

1 This essay is based on remarks I delivered at an online panel with Julia Azari, of Marquette University, and former Congressman Mickey Edwards, "The Role of Civility in Politics, Political Institutions, and Democracy," organized by the John Brademas Center of New York University, March 9, 2022, www.nyu.edu.

2 National Constitution Center, "On This Day: The First Bitter, Contested Presidential Election Takes Place," November 4, 2021, constitutioncenter.org.

3 Joanne B. Freeman, *Field of Blood* (Farrar, Straus & Giroux, 2018).

4 "President Franklin Roosevelt's Radio Address Unveiling the Second Half of the New Deal," October 31, 1936, www.archives.gov.

5 Lisa Romano, "Duel on the Hill," *Washington Post*, March 6, 1985.

6 Donald R. Matthews, *U.S. Senators and Their World* (University of North Carolina Press, 1960), 98–99.

7 From a pamphlet developed by GOPAC, "Language: A Key Mechanism of Control," uh.edu.

8 Sean M. Theriault, *The Gingrich Senators: The Roots of Partisan Warfare in Congress* (Oxford University Press, 2013).

9 Thomas E. Mann and Norman J. Ornstein, *It's Even Worse than It Looks* (Basic Books, 2012).

10 Survey Center on American Life, "After the Ballots are Counted: Conspiracies, Political Violence, and American Exceptionalism," February 11, 2021, www.americansurveycenter.org.

6

Civility at the Intersection of Presidential and Party Politics

JULIA AZARI

Incivility is a hallmark of the Trump era, and of the 45th president himself. What most visibly separated Trump from past presidential candidates was not the racism of his policies or his lack of political experience (just ask Wendell Wilkie or Ross Perot). It was the insults he directed at those who dared to challenge him. These insults—which often were racist or sexist—created a sense among commentators that Trump was fundamentally unpresidential. The definition, of course, had to be revised when Trump was elected to office in 2016. His election concluded an intensely negative and partisan campaign season, and ushered in more racial and political tension in a nation already divided.

Outrage about the decline of civility was not confined to Trump opponents. Allies of the 45th president also accused their opponents of being unable to take part in a civil debate. An especially prominent incident took place in the spring of 2018: after White House press secretary Sarah Huckabee Sanders was asked to leave a Virginia restaurant, commentators on the left and the right became embroiled in what *National Review*'s Karl Salzmann termed "the civility wars."[1] Rep. Maxine Waters (D-CA) encouraged supporters to confront in public members of the Trump administration—specifically, over their immigration policies—and to let them know that they are "not welcome anymore, anywhere."[2] Others, on the left and the right, maintained that public officials were entitled to civil treatment in public places.

Under these conditions, civility itself has become a contentious issue. Not everyone on the left side of the spectrum lamented the decline of civility, or associated it solely with Trump's crude insults. An alternative take on civility contends, as intimated in the conflict over Huckabee Sanders, that it is used to silence marginalized voices and to "tone police" demands for justice. NPR's Karen Grigsby-Bates reported on the use of charges of incivility to silence minority protest, such as NFL player Colin Kaepernick's decision to kneel during the national anthem before games. In other words, like everything else, we're polarized about the meaning of civility.[3]

In this brief essay, I explore the functions of civility as they relate to the evolution of modern presidential and party politics. Breaking down the concept this way and thinking about it in relation to changing aspects of politics can help us reconcile the two views about civility and understand how they coexist. I define civility very broadly—as norms about what kind of language and claims are acceptable in the course of standard political discourse. I conceptualize civility as a boundary, which, like all boundaries, can be both useful and corrosive.

Scholars of several fields, including political communication and political theory, have investigated the role of civility in democratic politics. I approach the topic as a scholar of institutions; namely, American political parties and the presidency. Through this lens, I identify three functions for civility in politics: to acknowledge the legitimacy of the opposition; to protect individuals; and to preserve power. The first two functions can serve or undermine the third, depending on the context.

Perhaps the most familiar of these functions is the role of civility in acknowledging political opponents and the right for opposing views to exist and contest political office. When Republicans and Democrats call each other names, impugn each other's motives, or question each other's right to participate in a space, they undermine the possibility that we can fight for a shared common good, despite our different views. An important question to ask is a temporal one: Does a decline in civility come before major clashes over policy, or does it come after? Does civility deepen the problem, or simply reflect the problem? Does uncivil language give the appearance of fundamental disagreement where none really exists? Or does civility mask existential disagreement? Our search for deeper answers to these questions can help us identify exactly what's going on.

The question of incivility speaks to some large—and empirical debates—in political psychology about the nature of polarization. One debate is whether polarized attitudes are driven by identity and psychological attachment to one's own "team," or by true ideological disagreements.[4] Mason's pathbreaking work on political polarization and social psychology invokes civility in its title, *Uncivil Agreement,* suggesting that the tone of conflict is central to the nature of that conflict. Decades of research also suggest that incivility shapes citizens' political perceptions, from depressing trust in government to alienating those who are conflict averse.[5]

Thinking about civility as a boundary that protects legitimate opposition also helps us understand how incivility works differently in the case of presidents. Trump's comments about journalists, legislators, and, perhaps most chillingly, the occasional private citizen engage different power dynamics than if they were coming from someone other than a president or presidential candidate. During the campaign, then-candidate Trump lashed out at a college student who criticized his record on gender, resulting in rape threats to her and other harassment.[6] Trump's verbal aggression to journalists similarly set a prominent example that his supporters were all too eager to follow; and, if rhetorically, insinuated the power of the state into efforts to silence criticism and scrutiny.

Although somewhat of a challenge to remember or recognize, after living through the Trump era, we note that tension around presidential language could also be observed during Obama's presidency. In some ways, it is easier to isolate the effects of language then, because it was not accompanied by Trump's theatrics—and his Twitter following. While not approaching Trump's level, Obama's sometimes casual language—the police "acted stupidly"; Kanye West is a "jackass"—mixed poorly with the presidency. As I've written, you can't call someone stupid when you have the nuclear codes, or at least not expect to ignite a strong reaction.[7]

Obama's tendency to use such language made possible Trump's style of communication, which played fast and loose with prescribed boundaries. Verbal sparring that would have been routine in regular debate takes on a different significance when it comes from the president of the United States. These communication tactics, when paired with an obvious power imbalance—the president of the United States versus nearly anyone else—help reveal how power shapes the context of civil and uncivil communication.

The informal rules of civility also exist to protect individuals from unfair and inappropriate attacks. After Press Secretary Sanders was asked to leave the restaurant in 2018, some pushback suggested that, despite political disagreements, those who work in politics should be allowed to live private lives. Similarly, among the many complaints Trump has leveled at the House Select Committee investigating the January 6, 2021, insurrection is that its members were "going after his children," because of the committee's interest in speaking to Ivanka Trump—who had, in fact, served as a close adviser to the president, her father.

These considerations are linked to two features of modern politics: candidate-centered elections and an omnipresent media environment. It is illuminating to compare today's political discourse to the language of the 19th century. Highly personal insults were not uncommon during presidential campaigns and political back-and-forth. Lincoln biographer David Herbert Donald notes that Democratic politicians referred to the 16th president as a "gorilla, baboon, and long-armed ape" and "suggested that the President had unmentionable diseases or that he had Negro blood in his veins."[8] The 1828 campaign featured criticisms of Andrew Jackson for his marriage to Rachel Donelson Robards Jackson, who had been married previously (and not officially divorced when she and Jackson married in 1791).[9] Rough political discourse from the past reveals the changing taboos in society. But civility seems to have taken on new importance as party machines waned, individual politicians became more significant, and politics became more saturated with new forms of media. As media gained the potential to expose more and more elements of politicians' lives, the norm of civility functioned to place aspects of their private lives, belief systems, and behavior off-limits. Media norms through the mid-20th century led journalists mostly to refrain from commenting on both the physical disabilities and extramarital affairs of Franklin Roosevelt and John F. Kennedy. The introduction first of television, then the 24-hour cable news cycle, then social media has allowed the public constant and intimate access to politicians. Expectations of civility—respect for out-of-bounds topics—offer an increasingly thin veneer of protection for politicians in such an environment.

When politics revolves around individuals, these norms of civility are meant to lower the costs of entering the competition. They protect core values: that family members, especially children, may not be drawn into political disputes. They draw a line between personal conduct and politics. But this line has been challenged—

often in the context of larger questions about social change. For example, norms of civility suggest that religion is off-limits as a subject of campaign taunts. But John F. Kennedy, Barack Obama, or Mitt Romney might see the issue differently.

These norms, too, produce a tension in contemporary politics: some highly personal topics still seem as if they should be off-limits. But as American politics has replaced a candidate-centered era with one in which we place less emphasis on specific individuals and greater emphasis on party affiliation and ideology, civility norms at the individual level can seem trite or beside the point. Even as Trump the individual has come to dominate the Republican party, partisan loyalty is often offered as an explanation for why the normal rules of politics, including civility, seem not to apply to him. And yet, at a time when we are starting to examine power dynamics—racial inequities, sexual harassment—private behavior has political relevance.

Finally, norms of civility can be invoked to protect the status quo and the existing power arrangements. This problem with civility and norms discourse has been well documented by scholars of social movements and protest, especially those focused on race. As Lynn Mie Itagaki observes, "The emotional labor of civility was more often extracted from vulnerable populations who had to repeatedly overlook microaggressions or be forced to 'cover'"—that is, behave like the dominant group or hide differences.[10] Broadly conceived norms of civility also preclude calling ideas or people racist, or drawing extreme comparisons (to Nazis or other authoritarians)—even when the stated ideas are egregious and the analogies justified by speech and behavior. One definition of civility suggests that "extreme characterizations of legislation" were considered uncivil. Hall Jamieson, Volinsky, Weitz, and Kensi offer the example of "saying senior citizens would die under the opposing side's health plan."[11] Other examples might include invoking the possibility of genocide, or extreme threats to bodily autonomy (like banning abortions for rape victims).

Yet extreme possibilities are sometimes an important part of the policy discussion. Health care policies can threaten lives, governments and armed groups commit genocide, and, as 2022 has shown, severe restrictions on abortion can be passed and enacted very quickly. Civility on its own does little to tell us when a claim is investigating unlikely but relevant implications, and when it is being used to inflame. The way in which civility creates boundaries around acceptable discourse intersects powerfully with its first function—to protect the legitimacy of opposition. As Teresa Bejan writes, calls for civility "suggest that if only we could get the manner right, the very practice of disagreement itself might work to harmonize our fundamental differences, thus making it possible for us to regard one another across those differences as not enemies, but friends."[12] But this objective is not always possible; sometimes, what one's opponent has said is indeed racist, sexist, or otherwise harmful. Or false.

This function of civility certainly can work to preserve political power, creating a feedback loop in which those who already enjoy power also enjoy the ability to police boundaries. Nevertheless, some lines probably need to exist: some questions need to be off-limits; some insults ought to be deemed too corrosive. What civility doesn't do is help us when the underlying values of the political community are in question. When it becomes a guideline for how to renegotiate those values, civility can be a tool for preserving power imbalances. Demands for inclusion or equal treatment can violate existing agreements about the bounds of political discourse.

What are the consequences of the three purposes of civility? First, they show how the concept of civility can encompass both principles that are necessary for democracy to function and those that keep it from improving. These features are reinforcing at times—not always at odds. The ways in which norms of civility uphold the idea of legitimate opposition also limit potentially necessary political conversations.

Second, they illustrate how civility evolves with the political context; how received expectations and norms can become stale and outdated. Norms from the candidate-centered era that placed private life and behavior off-limits may not mesh well with contemporary concerns.

Civility norms not only reflect changing political conditions; they also play a role in creating political change. After a politician or a political party violates these expectations, what happens next is shaped by what the other side does. We can gain some leverage on understanding how the concept of civility works by looking at it as a dynamic, moving boundary, serving multiple functions, rather than a single concept with a fixed definition.

NOTES

1 Karl J. Salzmann, "The Civility Wars," *National Review*, July 10, 2018, www.nationalreview.com.

2 Jennifer Calfas, "'They're Not Welcome Anymore, Anywhere': Maxine Waters Tells Supporters to Confront Trump Officials," *Time*, June 25, 2018, time.com.

3 Karen Grigsby Bates, "When Civility Is Used as a Cudgel Against People of Color," NPR, March 14, 2019, www.npr.org.

4 For elaboration of the identity position, see Lilliana Mason, *Uncivil Agreement: How Politics Became Our Identity* (University of Chicago Press, 2018); and Lilliana Mason and Julie Wronski, "One Tribe to Bind Them All: How Our Social Group Attachments Strengthen Partisanship," *Political Psychology* 39, no. S1 (February 2018): 257–77. For elaboration of the ideology position, see Steven W. Webster and Alan I. Abramowitz, "The Ideological Foundations of Affective Polarization in the U.S. Electorate," *American Politics Research* 45, no. 4 (July 2017): 621–47; and Yphtach Lelkes, "Affective Polarization and Ideological Sorting: A Reciprocal, Albeit Weak, Relationship," *The Forum* 16, no. 1 (April 2018): 67–79.

5 Diana C. Mutz and Byron Reeves, "The New Videomalaise: Effects of Televised Incivility on Political Trust," *American Political Science Review* 99, no. 1 (February 2005): 1–15; Emily Sydnor, *Disrespectful Democracy: The Psychology of Political Incivility* (Columbia University Press, 2019).

6 Emma Sarran Webster, "A College Student Received Rape Threats After Donald Trump Shamed Her on Twitter," *Teen Vogue*, December 9, 2016, www.teenvogue.com.

7 Julia Azari, "Obama's Communication Legacy," *Juncture* 23, no. 3 (2016): 143–45.

8 David Herbert Donald, "A. Lincoln, Politician," in *Lincoln Reconsidered: Essays on the Civil War* (Vintage, 2001).

9 Donald B. Cole, *Vindicating Andrew Jackson: The 1828 Election and the Rise of the Two-Party System* (University Press of Kansas, 2009), 78.

10 Lynn Mie Itagaki, "The Long Con of Civility," *Connecticut Law Review* 52, no. 3 (2021): 1169–86. See also Tali Mendelberg, "Deliberation, Incivility, and Race in Electoral Campaigns," *Democratization in America: A Comparative-Historical Analysis* (Johns Hopkins University Press, 2009), 157–83; and Kenji Yoshino, *Covering: The Hidden Assault on Our Civil Rights* (Random House, 2011).

11 Kathleen Hall Jamieson, Allyson Volinsky, Ilana Weitz, and Kate Kenski, "The Political Uses and Abuses of Civility and Incivility," *The Oxford Handbook of Political Communication*, 2017, academic.oup.com, 205–18.

12 Teresa M. Bejan, *Mere Civility* (Harvard University Press, 2017), 6.

7

The Politics of Performance

MICHAEL F. DINISCIA

Introduction

In the United States today, we are suffering from a crisis of the "politics of performance." Politicking by members of Congress that for decades was conducted behind closed doors and out of the eye of the everyday voter is now on display 24–7 on cable and news websites and social media. This phenomenon has been occurring in the context of a polarized electorate, with control of the White House and Congress coming down to mere tens of thousands of votes. At the same time, legislating power within Congress has become concentrated in the hands of each chamber's leadership at the expense of committees and individual representatives and senators. These elements incentivize performative politics—prioritizing communications, media presence, and personal branding over the nuts and bolts of legislating.

Much of this political posturing includes increasingly uncivil rhetoric, with serious consequences for the ability of Congress to address the pressing issues facing our nation. Politics is inherently conflictual, and our separation of powers system was designed not merely to manage conflict, but to channel it to productive ends. Yet the effective functioning of this system depends on a degree of civility among political actors. If political discourse devolves into rhetoric that calls into question the legitimacy and patriotism of opponents, how can lawmakers sit down together to forge legislative compromises?

Setting the Stage

In a democracy, citizens and their representatives are in competition not only over their interests, but also their values and vision for the country, inevitably stirring intense passions in pursuit of political goals. In his autobiography and treatise on American history and politics, the historian Henry Adams (great-grandson of John Adams and grandson of John Quincy Adams) declared "politics, as a practice, whatever its professions, had always been the systematic organization of hatreds."[1] The founders and leaders who followed them have built institutions of government and politics to manage conflict and promote compromise in order to prevent the system from spiraling into dysfunction and violence (although, as the Civil War attests, this effort has not always been successful).[2]

Contemporary voters, however, tend not to recognize conflict as intrinsic to democracy and fail to appreciate the Constitution's productive channeling of it. Instead, voters often express negative views of the very presence of conflict in politics. For example, a 2023 Pew Research Center survey found that "more than eight-in-ten Americans (86%) say the following is a good description of politics: 'Republicans and Democrats are more focused on fighting each other than on solving problems.'"[3] Citizens expressing this view may genuinely see conflict itself as negative and would favor a system that encourages consensus and moderation in legislating. Or, just as likely, they may be blaming the presence of partisan conflict, and not institutions' deficiencies in managing it, for the failure of the political system to produce outcomes that reflect their policy preferences—especially when their desired policies lie closer to either end of the ideological spectrum rather than in the middle. When voters opine that they want Democrats and Republicans in Washington to come together and do what's right for the American people, they do not often mean compromises where one side of the aisle gets a partial loaf and the other side may get half or an even larger portion. Instead, they expect politicians to set aside their partisan differences and agree on the exact policy position the individual voter supports. What that voter ignores, of course, is that other citizens who also profess a desire for lawmakers to stop fighting and do the right thing may hold diametrically opposed policy preferences.

While consensus may be the lifeblood of the norms that guide democracy, compromise is essential for generating the outcomes a functioning democratic government should deliver. Thus, the Constitution created a separation of powers federal system, and American political institutions evolved over two and a half centuries to channel conflict into compromise and legislation. Voters today, however, are not entirely wrong in their negative views of disagreement and political fighting. Our institutions have become less effective in managing conflict and delivering significant legislation, even when one party controls both houses of Congress and the White House (although Democrats have been more successful than Republicans in the same situation). Politicians appear more interested in fighting for reasons of tribal loyalty and tactical advantage, content with leaving the status quo in place even in the face of mounting global challenges. Much of this change can be attributed, I will argue, to a rise in a more parliamentary-style, nationalized partisan politics and the decline in the use of nonpublic spaces by lawmakers for the core functions of policymaking. Voters nevertheless share in the blame if they keep electing and reelecting those members of Congress who pursue the politics of performance and electorally punish others who prioritize legislative compromise.

This transformation is taking place in the context of growing political polarization in the United States. While polarization is not a new occurrence, its intensity seems to be exponentially increasing. As Princeton University political scientist Frances Lee describes it in her book *Insecure Majorities: Congress and the Perpetual Campaign*, for the past two decades Americans have been living with a winner-take-all, knife's-edge politics, where small changes in the electorate produce significant swings in political power.[4] Rather than promoting moderation and consensus in an attempt to capture the middle and build larger electoral coalitions, Lee argues the parties have been incentivized to pursue strategies of negative partisanship and political messaging, which increase base turnout and dampen enthusiasm among the other party's voters, adding to polarization.

Ironically, one reason political fighting has become so intense is that the stakes can, from a certain perspective, seem so low. When Congress writes the federal budget each year, statutes and politics limit how much spending is effectively up for grabs. Most (although not all) members of both parties will not touch Social Security, Medicare, and the Department of Defense in the annual budget fight. Since entitlements and other mandatory programs (not including Medicaid), defense spending, and interest payments on the national debt constitute nearly 75 percent of the federal budget and are in essence on autopilot, Congress is left to fight over only one-quarter of the budget each year.[5] Yet even that underestimates the popularity and durability of much of discretionary spending (such as Affordable Care Act subsidies). Thus, the tiny percentage of the annual budget where expenditures are adjusted, removed, or added takes on greater political significance. One result is that smaller budget items like funding the National Endowment for the Arts and foreign aid, which have greater partisan salience, become easy targets for major fights. This practical budget constraint also raises the prominence of debates in Congress over other social and cultural issues, which don't involve spending, as well as the visibility of Senate confirmation fights over executive branch and judicial nominations.

Polarized Politics in a Separation of Powers System

Politics in the United States is taking on characteristics more often found in a parliamentary democracy. Voters are becoming more partisan (even if they aren't necessarily more ideological) and voting by party more than candidate; parties and their candidates are increasingly reliant on small-dollar donors, who are more akin to the dues-paying membership of a British political party; weaker competition in general elections is increasing the importance of primaries in determining final electoral outcomes; and the legislative process has become dominated by congressional leadership instead of committees.

There are numerous factors contributing to this state of affairs: party strategies that elevate negative partisanship and the nationalizing of elections; changes in how Americans get news and information; new ways politicians can reach voters and raise campaign funds; and institutional changes in Congress. Yet, as the Marquette University political scientist Julia Azari contends, "the defining characteristic of our moment is that parties are weak while partisanship is strong."[6] In a true parliamentary system with strong parties, party leadership can discipline individual members by withholding resources (campaign funds, TV airtime, legislative staff) or by stripping a member of a coveted committee slot. But in the US, with weak parties as Azari defines them, candidates and sitting members of Congress are less dependent on leadership for resources and therefore feel unleashed to build their own brands through the politics of performance. In doing so, they can also drive how the public sees the parties and perceives their agendas.

No other Democrats in the House joined Cori Bush in her call to "defund the police," yet four years later that phrase was still haunting Democratic candidates.[7]

This slide into the politics of performance begins with elections and campaigns. For a variety of reasons, but especially because of the centrality to the American story of the decades-long struggles for women's suffrage and voting rights for African Americans, elections have been seen as the "one and done" of democracy. In a winner-take-all, two-party system, citizens see an election in which they take part every two to four years, rather than ongoing civic engagement, as the way to achieve their political goals. Elections are viewed as existentially consequential, leaving partisans who supported the losing candidates angry and even fearful of being shut out. Even those who supported the winning candidates will be disappointed when, once in office, those candidates inevitably fail to deliver on every extravagant campaign promise.

Yet when it comes to Congress, most of the electorate has little choice in the general election because of gerrymandered districts combined with a natural sorting of the parties along rural and urban lines. From a high in 1978 of 173 districts with a partisan voting index (PVI, a commonly accepted indicator of the electoral competitiveness of a congressional district) of Republican or Democrat +5 or less, there were only 86 such districts by 2024. And in that election, the nonpartisan analysts of the Cook Political Report (the original developers of PVI) rated only 27 out of 435 total seats in the House as genuine tossups.[8] Most representatives are effectively elected during the congressional primaries. And primaries are notoriously low in turnout; for example, in New York in 2024, only 15 percent of registered voters cast ballots on average across the state.[9] One consequence is that more ideologically extreme—or, in the context of the politics of performance, "performatively" extreme—candidates can capture nominations and go on to win the general election.

Control of the House of Representatives comes down to a handful of races (with some of the smallest majorities in the House occurring in recent years), along with a half-dozen swing states at the Senate and presidential level. In 2024, even Donald Trump's victory in the Electoral College was decided by fewer than 250,000 votes in three states, out of a total 154 million votes cast nationwide. But, as Frances Lee argues, this knife's-edge electoral politics hasn't pushed the parties toward the middle, but has fomented partisanship, and in particular a negative partisanship designed to motivate the maximum turnout of base voters and to dampen turnout of the opposition's voters.[10] In the 1990s, Newt Gingrich pioneered not just the nationalization of congressional elections with the Republicans' "Contract with America," but also the negative partisanship strategy of painting members of the opposing party as everything from corrupt to a threat to America.[11]

This style of negative partisanship, with its inherent incivility, may prove an effective short-term electoral strategy, but it has failed to build lasting electoral coalitions. As the legal scholar Jedediah Purdy writes in his book *Two Cheers for Politics*, "Few elections result in the sweeping legislation that builds new constituencies and lasting majorities as the social protections of the New Deal did. So campaigns have shifted into a symbolic and defensive mode. The way to mobilize voters is not to promise a better world, but to impress on them the urgency of keeping the other candidate and party out of power."[12]

Unlike in a parliamentary system, institutions in the US system are designed to empower political minorities—the Senate filibuster rule, the Electoral College, and the potential for divided government. Because we no longer have a dominant party at either the presidential or congressional level, the party out of power has less incentive to cooperate on legislation. Instead, it can make gains in the next electoral cycle largely by blocking and hampering policymaking, rendering the party that controls the levers of power seem ineffective. As City College of New York political scientist Daniel DiSalvo asserts, "Party unity today is more about political messaging than legislating. Given the relatively slim and unstable majorities in either chamber of Congress over the last 25 years, every election cycle holds out the false hope that, by vigorously opposing everything the other party does, one's own party will someday run the table and be able to enact its policy program. The result is higher party-unity scores—along with legislative gridlock."[13]

Irregular Order in Congress

The past three decades have also witnessed significant changes in how the House and Senate operate. In their books *The Broken Branch* and *It's Even Worse than It Looks*, the longtime scholars of Congress Tom Mann and Norman Ornstein comprehensively chronicle the breakdown in what had been considered regular order.[14] They detail everything from the abuse of holding House floor votes open beyond their allotted time to the overreliance on omnibus bills and continuing resolutions for the federal budget.

In particular, Mann and Ornstein lay out how the leadership offices in the House and Senate have concentrated legislative policymaking power in their own hands at the expense of committees.[15] This tactic may seem more efficient from the vantage point of the speaker's suite—or even the only option under current conditions to keep the legislative process moving and the government paying its bills. But for much of congressional history, seniority and committee assignments were the currency. Representatives and senators built up expertise in the hard grind of drafting legislation. Committee and subcommittee chairs held the levers of legislative power—the subcommittee chairs of the House appropriations committee were famously referred to as "the cardinals." But patiently working their way up the ladder no longer guarantees members influence in crafting bills. At the same time, the increase in polarization and decline in regular order has resulted in greater reliance on the reconciliation process and "must pass" omnibus and minibus bills, with less room for other serious legislation. It means, as Daniel DiSalvo points out, that more of the bills proposed—regardless of their chances for passage—are designed for political messaging to voters.

Under these circumstances, rank-and-file members and committee and subcommittee chairs are incentivized to be "show horses," not "workhorses," in congressional parlance.[16] This show-horse politics of performance plays out in the prominence of committee hearings for investigations or confirmations of executive branch and judicial nominations (as opposed to hearings for drafting bills). Hectoring of witnesses and outlandish statements from the dais have become de rigueur, as members jockey for attention and sound bites that will land on television or go viral on social media.

Perhaps nothing so starkly illustrates the politics of performance and breakdown in civility as an exchange at a Senate Health, Education, Labor, and Pensions Committee hearing in 2023. The heated back and forth transpired between a Republican senator from Oklahoma, Markwayne Mullin, and Sean O'Brien, president of the International Brotherhood of Teamsters. It quickly devolved to the point where Senator Mullins essentially challenged O'Brien to a physical fight: "This is a time, this is a place. If you want to run your mouth, we can be two consenting adults. We can finish it here."[17]

Comity across the aisle is another casualty of the decline in regular order. With a breakdown in the legislative work of committees, the chair and ranking member, let alone other more junior members, no longer work intensively together. In an interview with *The New York Times*, the moderate Republican senator from Maine, Susan Collins, discusses one of the consequences. "When we had a strong committee system, you had strong relationships based on trust between the chairman and ranking member. . . . Now, because the committee structure and the power of the committees has lessened and more and more legislation is written either by groups like ours [an ad hoc group of senators that drafted the Bipartisan Infrastructure Law of 2021] or in the leader's office, it is harder to build those bonds of trust that allow you to get things done."[18]

The lack of cross-party relationships makes it easier to vilify members of the opposing party. It leads to the more intense adversarial nature of committee hearings, as well as the production of messaging bills designed to embarrass the opposition with tough votes, hurting its electoral chances in the next cycle.

Too Much Exposure

It is not just the breakdown in regular order that has led to the politics of performance in Congress. Ironically, several good government reforms over past decades have contributed to this phenomenon. These reforms have often focused on making Congress and the legislative process more transparent. Yet by taking away the so-called "smoke-filled backrooms"—spaces where traditional politicking and compromise took place—the reforms have had the unintended consequence of making Congress less productive.[19]

One such reform was the introduction of C-SPAN. "A nonprofit created in 1979 by a then-new industry called cable television," the network was envisioned as "providing gavel-to-gavel coverage of the workings of the US Congress . . . without editing, commentary or analysis."[20] By 1984, a then-Republican backbencher realized he could exploit this channel, which was televising directly from the House floor. As Princeton historian Julian Zelizer chronicles in his book *Burning Down the House: Newt Gingrich, the Fall of a Speaker, and the Rise of the New Republican Party*, Gingrich took advantage of the fact that the C-SPAN camera was fixed in place to capture the podium from which a representative would be making a speech. The television picture did not show the rest of floor—which was usually empty at the end of the day, when Gingrich would choose to make his remarks. As Gingrich would accuse Democrats of corruption, even singling out some members of the House by name and daring them to respond, a C-SPAN viewer could be forgiven for thinking the Democratic members had been shamed into silence, when in fact they were never there.[21]

Another transparency reform that gave rise to the politics of performance was the elimination of teller votes. Unless a resolution could be passed by unanimous consent or a voice vote, the House recorded how representatives voted only on a final bill. The clerk of the House would not, however, usually record how each member voted on amendments to those bills. Representatives would instead cast amendment votes by walking up and down the aisles and announcing to one of their party's deputy whips, or "tellers," whether they were voting for or against. The deputy whips would record the total ayes and nays, but not which one each member cast. In a push for transparency, the Legislative Reorganization Act of 1970 ended that practice. As a *New York Times* article at the time of its passage described it, "The move . . . would require that members be recorded by name as they passed up the aisle to vote on amendments. Members are currently counted, but not recorded by name, on such votes on amendments, known as teller votes. Members' votes on key issues were thus cloaked in secrecy, and critics long contended that constituents had a right to know how their representatives had voted."[22] In their book *The Broken Branch,* Mann and Ornstein explain how ending the use of teller voters helped lead to an increase in amendments offered for the purpose of political messaging, forcing members of the opposing party to take votes that could be used against them at the next election.[23]

These transparency reforms are not the only way members of Congress and their actions have become increasingly visible to the public. We have also witnessed over the past four decades an explosion in coverage of politics and politicians by national news media. This coverage was pioneered by the original 24-7 cable news channels—CNN, Fox News, and MSNBC. But, as the internet took off in the late 1990s, they were eventually joined by online news sites such as Politico or the HuffPost on the left and the Drudge Report on the right. Recently, we've seen even more cable news startups (some extremely partisan, like OAN) along with a proliferation of politics podcasts.

This media landscape has meant that journalists can dig more deeply into Capitol Hill and share with audiences how the sausage is made. Because cable networks need to fill airtime, they also offer lawmakers an opportunity to appear live and engage in performative politics. What often holds the most appeal for audiences is partisan conflict. A 2023 study conducted by the Center for Media and Public Affairs at George Mason University analyzed coverage of members of Congress by broadcast networks, cable news, and online news sites.[24] What the study found is that hyperpartisan members received over four times the amount of coverage as their bipartisan colleagues.[25] Senators and representatives who want to reach a national audience and build name recognition are incentivized to pick partisan fights and ratchet up their rhetoric.

Social media amplifies this trend. Clips of lawmakers' performances on cable news programs can go viral on TikTok and X: the more partisan or confrontational the clip, the more likely it will take off. Politicians can also directly or through influencers reach out on social media to grab voters' attention—and their campaign contributions. Again, the more provocative a member sounds, the more followers accrue.

But if legislating is not their goal, how are these lawmakers who populate cable news and social media defining political victory? In a 2023 opinion essay in *The New York Times,* the democracy scholar Yuval Levin argues that victory has come "to mean winning a prominent platform for performative outrage, where you can articulate your voters' frustrations with elite power, and show them that you are working to disrupt the uses of that power." Furthermore, "members respond to the incentives of political theater, which is often at least as well served by legislative failure as success. This impulse is evident in both parties, though it is clearly most intense among a portion of congressional Republicans."[26]

Uncivil Rhetoric and Its Consequences

Citizens often take their cues from political elites. As members of Congress ramp up their combative and heated language on the floors of the House and Senate, on television, and in social media, what is the impact on broader public discourse in the United States? In the most extreme case, as we learned on January 6, 2021, when then-President Donald Trump exhorted his followers to "fight like hell," violent rhetoric can lead to physical violence.

At the very least, the politics of performance is contributing to a growing incivility in how Americans view their politics. A 2021 poll from the Public Religion Research Institute found that 30 percent of Republican respondents agreed that "because things have gotten so far off track, true American patriots may have to resort to violence in order to save our country."[27] The sentiment is not limited to Republicans. A 2022 poll from CBS News and YouGov showed that roughly half of Democrats viewed Republicans not as political opponents but as "enemies."[28]

Multiple incidents in recent years illustrate how viewing political opponents as enemies can develop into threats of violence against politicians and other citizens. Among the examples are the harassment election workers have endured; school boards that had to curb public comments after meetings devolved into shouting matches; and even the Congressional Management Foundation's warning to lawmakers not to hold open public meetings out of security concerns.[29] The worry here is that, like January 6, as violent language becomes a normalized part of discourse, it more likely tips into violent acts.

Conclusion

If we desire a more functional Congress, can we change incentives to promote civility and compromise? We are unlikely to rein in the worst effects of cable news and social media anytime soon. Further advances in AI may prove an accelerant to our political fires. But senators and representatives do set the rules for their own chambers. Perhaps they can adopt some institutional changes to help turn down the heat. In the current political climate these ideas may seem like small-bore solutions, yet even they would mark an improvement over recent years.

Several reforms proposed by good government advocates, as well as by many former members of Congress, offer ways to encourage lawmakers to spend more time together, especially with colleagues across the aisle. One idea that regularly comes up is to lengthen the congressional workweek. Another is to break up committees—increasing their number and reducing their sizes. A third would be to require that the composition of congressional delegations for foreign travel be more bipartisan.[30]

Members of Congress can also look for ways to do more of their legislating out of the public eye. This change would require that the news media and the public accept less transparency—admittedly a tall order. By denying our politicians private space to do some of the work of legislating, we have pushed them into the politics of performance. If we truly want roll back the coarsening of political discourse and have a more functioning Congress, we should consider bringing back some of those old (at least metaphorically) smoke-filled backrooms.

NOTES

1 Henry Adams, *The Education of Henry Adams* (Houghton Mifflin, 1907).

2 See, for example, Lee Drutman, *Breaking the Two-Party Doom Loop: The Case for Multiparty Democracy in America* (Oxford University Press, 2020), 123–56.

3 "Americans' Dismal Views of the Nation's Politics," Pew Research Center, September 19, 2023, www.pewresearch.org.

4 Frances Lee, *Insecure Majorities: Congress and the Perpetual Campaign* (University of Chicago Press, 2016).

5 "Policy Basics: Introduction to the Federal Budget Process," Center on Budget and Policy Priorities, www.cbpp.org.

6 Julia Azari, "Weak Parties and Strong Partisanship Are a Bad Combination," Vox, November 3, 2016, www.vox.com.

7 Andrew Kaczynski and Em Steck, "Kamala Harris Praised 'Defund the Police' Movement in June 2020 Radio Interview," CNN, July 7, 2024, www.cnn.com.

8 "The Competitive Districts That Will Decide Control of the House," Brennan Center for Justice, September 24, 2024, www.brennancenter.org.

9 Kate Lisa, "Low N.Y. Primary Turnout Spurs Calls to Increase Voters, Ballot Access," Spectrum News 1, July 1, 2024, spectrumlocalnews.com.

10 See, for example, Alan I. Abramowitz and Steven W. Webster, "Negative Partisanship: Why Americans Dislike Parties but Behave Like Rabid Partisans," *Political Psychology* 39, no. S1 (February 1, 2018): 119–35; Chris Lehmann, "The Power of Negative Thinking," *The Nation*, November 21, 2022, www.thenation.com; and Charlie Cook, "The Power of 'Negative Partisanship,'" Cook Political Report, April 19, 2019, www.cookpolitical.com.

11 As early as a June 24, 1978, speech to the College Republicans at the Atlanta Airport Holiday Inn, Gingrich declared: "I think that one of the great problems we have in the Republican Party is that we don't encourage you to be nasty. We encourage you to be neat, obedient, and loyal and faithful and all those Boy Scout words, which would be great around the camp fire, but are lousy in politics." From "The Long March of Newt Gingrich," PBS FRONTLINE, November 18, 2015, www.pbs.org.

12 Jedediah Purdy, *Two Cheers for Politics*, (Basic Books, 2022).

13 Daniel DiSalvo, "Party Factions and American Politics," *National Affairs* 52 (Summer 2022), www.nationalaffairs.com.

14 Thomas E. Mann and Norman J. Ornstein, *The Broken Branch: How Congress Is Failing America and How to Get It Back on Track* (Oxford University Press, 2006); Thomas E. Mann and Norman J. Ornstein, *It's Even Worse than It Looks: How the American Constitutional System Collided with the New Politics of Extremism* (Basic Books, 2016).

15 A phenomenon quantified by three scholars at Harvard University through an analysis of campaign contributions and newspaper coverage. See Pamela Ban, Daniel Moskowitz, and James M. Snyder, "Leadership Power in Congress, 1890–2014: Evidence from PAC Contributions and Newspaper Coverage," *SSRN Electronic Journal*, January 1, 2016, papers.ssrn.com.

16 D. G. Martin, "*The Congressional Experience* Details Difference Between Political Workhorse and Show Horse," *Robesonian*, February 18, 2021, www.robesonian.com.

17 Monica Hesse, "Lawmaker Dudes Are Getting Kinda Fight-y," *Washington Post*, November 14, 2023, www.washingtonpost.com.

18 Carl Hulse, "Why Trust Is in Short Supply on Capitol Hill," *New York Times*, August 1, 2021, www.nytimes.com.

19 For an analysis of the decline in Congress's productivity as measured by the number of laws passed, see Moira Warburton and Ally J. Levine, "US Congress Is Getting Less Productive," Reuters, March 12, 2024, www.reuters.com, as well as original "legislative effectiveness data" compiled by the Center for Effective Lawmaking (a joint project of the University of Virginia and Vanderbilt University), thelawmakers.org.

20 "Our History," C-SPAN, www.c-span.org.

21 Julian Zelizer, *Burning Down the House: Newt Gingrich, the Fall of a Speaker, and the Rise of the New Republican Party* (Penguin, 2021) 62–70.

22 Marjorie Hunter, "House Backs End of Teller Votes on Amendments," *New York Times*, July 28, 1970, www.nytimes.com.

23 Mann and Ornstein, *Broken Branch*, 56.

24 "Change the Coverage," Starts with Us, March 13, 2024, startswith.us/changethecoverage.

25 Hyperpartisan and bipartisan members were identified using rankings from the Common Ground Scorecard: commongroundscorecard.org.

26 Yuval Levin, "What We Can Do to Make American Politics Less Dysfunctional," *New York Times*, October 9, 2023, www.nytimes.com.

27 "Competing Visions of America: An Evolving Identity or a Culture Under Attack? Findings From the 2021 American Values Survey," Public Religion Research Institute, January 11, 2021, www.prri.org.

28 Anthony Salvanto, "Americans Increasingly Concerned About Political Violence—CBS News Poll," CBS News, September 5, 2022, www.cbsnews.com.

29 See Christine Zhu, "Threats, Harassment of Election Workers Have Risen, Poll Shows," Politico, May 1, 2024, www.politico.com; Andrew Atterbury and Juan Perez Jr., "'Threats of Violence': School Boards Curb Public Comments to Calm Raucous Meetings," Politico, October 27, 2021, www.politico.com; and Lisa Lerer and Astead W. Herndon, "Menace Enters the Republican Mainstream," *New York Times*, November 12, 2021, www.nytimes.com.

30 For an analysis of how CODELs have become more partisan over the past four decades, see Zachary A. McGee and Sean M. Theriault, "Partisanship in Congressional Travels Abroad," *International Politics* 59, no. 5 (January 21, 2022): 925–54.

8

More than Manners

The Urgent Case for Civility

MICKEY EDWARDS

America is at an inflection point: major elements of our liberal democracy are under attack—respect for the outcome of elections, truthfulness, trust in the press and the courts. And with our democracy teetering, so, too, is the American republic—the structural and institutional framework designed to ensure justice, honor equality, serve the common good, and empower the majority without trampling the equal rights of nonmajorities. Our laws, our rules, and our norms are under challenge. America, a nation woven from the cultural and economic diversity of its states, had a natural motto: *e pluribus unum*. Out of many, one. But *unum*—the thread of common purpose that held these separate and semisovereign communities together—is increasingly difficult to find.

Given such a dire framework to work with, why does something as minor-sounding as "civility"—niceness and good manners—matter?

Let's look at some important numbers. Fifty. Three thousand and ninety. Three hundred and thirty million. Forty-eight million. Fifty states. Three thousand and ninety counties, parishes, and boroughs. Three hundred and thirty million people. Forty-eight million immigrants, from almost every country in the world. That's the United States.

We are not Norway. More than three centuries of immigration have greatly increased America's diversity. Even that tally of 48 million immigrants is misleading: add to it the children and grandchildren of immigrants—our friends and neighbors and work colleagues and fellow students and the tens of thousands, hundreds of thousands who live in the same city as you, the same state. My grandparents spoke Yiddish and brought with them the culture and norms of the shtetls of Europe. Others brought the customs and beliefs and religions of Peru or Laos or Kenya. There is assimilation, but assimilation does not erase the traditions and practices of one's past; it only adds another layer, a common feeling of being American. It's true that diverse backgrounds and experiences can also lead to different approaches to politics or cultural norms, and that those differences—the areas where there is less commonality—can put a strain on attempts to forge common purpose. Thus, the need to talk together, reason together, and work together to find the areas of overlapping interests.

In a nation as large and diverse as ours, that's not always easy. How can we make it work? Isn't "civility" much too small a thing to help us bridge these divides?

Civility is not, however, just "niceness" or "good manners" or "tolerance." It's something deeper. It's respect—respect for the humanity of even those with whom we disagree most ardently and are most determined to defeat. It's a shared openness—at least a willingness to listen without simultaneously forming a rebuttal; not just listening, but hearing. And it's restraint. Not every thought that pops into your head needs to come shooting out of your mouth.

Civility may be a nice thing in and of itself, and it's not all that hard to achieve. Even in totalitarian states, people can be nice to each other, respectful, kind. That's simply a mark of recognizing fellow humanness. In America, however—America the large,

America the diverse, America the divided—civility, respect, and restraint are democracy's lifeblood. There are too many of us, and we have too many differences. If we allow ourselves to be defined by where we diverge, our democracy will die.

But civility must come from within, right? Or be imbued from childhood. Taught at the mother's knee. Learned under the withering glare of someone respected.

In fact, civility can be—and must be—enforced by rules. Even adult humans can continue to learn. I'm a pretty casual guy. I shorten names and give people nicknames; I slouch, and sometimes perch on the edge of the desk for casual conversation. I'm more comfortable, more myself, in jeans than in a suit, and I hate neckties. But when I was first elected to Congress, I learned quickly that conforming to different behaviors was not a matter of choice. Among my new colleagues were friends—people I played golf with, whose homes I visited, whose children I knew. Nothing would have been more natural to me than to have engaged with these friends—and others who were now my colleagues—in the same breezy ways I always had. Yet, I could no longer jump into a conversation when John or Glenn or Nancy was speaking. I had to rise, stand at a microphone, and ask politely if they would yield the floor to me. And I had to address them, friends or not, as the gentleman or gentlelady from Illinois—or wherever else they came from. No jeans or sports shirts. While those strictures were slightly (and only slightly) relaxed over time, decorum was as enforced on the House floor as in the most posh private clubs of the elite.

We had an even greater number of cultural norms, enforced not by rule but by habit. Members of Congress did not help challengers campaign against other members of Congress: party solidarity was all fine, if you're into that sort of thing (which I'm not), but the guiding principle was the need to maintain enough mutual respect to be able to work with, negotiate with, and compromise with colleagues, whose right to be there and to represent their constituents and their conscience was the equal of my own.

These norms addressed the first reality I spoke of: our differences. No matter how great those differences, or how strongly we felt about our own views, with a Congress of 535 members, a presidency with veto powers, and courts prepared to step in if we crossed a constitutional line, nothing could happen—no spending on health care or national defense or public education, no authorization of agency initiatives, no appointment of judges or top military commanders—unless we could sit down together, talk to each other, trust one another.

Civility is the tape, the glue, the solder; the connective tissue that allows a vast, diverse democracy to work.

Tocqueville, in writing about this relatively new United States he visited in the early 1800s, found what he thought was the key to our success—the web of institutions and associations that brought us all together. Frederick Turner wrote about the American frontier and how it led to a new sense of confidence. In teaching my students about the works of Tocqueville and Turner, I noted that while the mindset of the American West strengthened a sense of independence and individuality, the real frontier also erased old-world hierarchies and gave rise to a rougher environment, in which mutuality was essential. Rousseau didn't create the social contract; it came to life organically from a world of interdependence. People had to stick together or fall separately. That condition meant a world in which one's word had to be given with serious intent, and trust had to be earned and expected. My hometown of Oklahoma City was erected in a single night in 1889—individuals staking out private claims, but then coming together to build a town, a city, a state.

None of that happens without strangers joining together, nor does it happen without the basics of civility—the key to building a community and now the key to ensuring that a nation, and a democracy, can survive.

Unfortunately, there's not a civility tree from which we can pick the fruit and, in eating it, change our fractious pastiche of certitude-laden communities into a singular national family with the advantages of familial love. And if there were such a tree, we don't have the luxury of waiting for it to reach maturity and provide its magical potion. Incivility—disrespect, distrust, an inability to get past an either/or, winner/loser calculus—will result not in pouting and surliness but in the destruction of the United States as a functional democracy.

Many critics of American government argue that democracy is not just messy, it's dysfunctional. That belief leads them to conclude that our constitutional system just doesn't work and is beyond repair. Such despair results in proposals for remedies like "ranked choice voting," which eliminates the need to determine the actual first choice of a majority of voters; or an 800-member House of Representatives, which would make the legislative branch too unwieldy to function and inevitably result in strengthening the executive and moving the United States into a de facto parliamentary system, with no serious separation of powers.

But our democratic system is not dysfunctional. True, it's not working as it should, but it's the very opposite of dysfunctional: the problem is that it's all too functional; it's operating exactly as it was designed to operate, not by the Constitution but by the electoral and governing structures we've created since, which have distorted and dismantled the hybrid democracy/republic system the Founders so carefully constructed.

By "functionality," I mean "operating according to design" (a car's engine starting up when you turn a key, a TV turning on when you press a button). The good news is that if the hatreds that block meaningful attempts at political deliberation and compromise are at least partly traceable to the political system we've fashioned, the problem is fixable; we need only change the controls to produce a better outcome.

So how do we change the political system in a way that will reduce the temperature, take away the fuel of competing warrior tribes, and rebuild the sense of community and the habits of civility? In a large and diverse nation, there will always be areas of strong disagreement, but how can we regain the ability to deal civilly with dissent and build bridges, rather than widening the gulf?

Here's one way. The republic the Founders conceived did not provide for political parties, which was a major break from the prevailing governing systems in Europe. In fact, the Constitution very specifically rejected parliamentary government by prohibiting simultaneous service in both the executive and legislative branches, and by requiring that members of Congress be actual inhabitants of the states from which they were elected. In this new nation, members of Congress were to represent constituencies (citizens), not political parties.

Today, however, the political parties as they currently operate in the United States, empowered by state laws that give them, in effect, control over both elections and governance, limit voters' choices, use primaries to weed out candidates who aren't sufficiently loyal to a partisan agenda, and too often elect candidates hostile to deliberation, compromise, mutual respect, and civility.

One way to bring back a sense of commonality and collective enterprise is to modify the way we allow political parties to operate. Parties, or some equivalent, are important in providing means to project dissent from prevailing opinion (or from views prevalent among elected officials). But we have taken the idea of parties to a strange extreme, giving them not only the ability to marshal support for or opposition to candidates and policies, but—by granting them the power through party primaries and attendant laws that keep primary losers off the general election ballot—allowing them to limit our choices at the ballot box to those favored by partisan insiders. Those laws can be changed.

Currently, inside the legislatures—both the national Congress and state legislative bodies—a party that has more of its members elected than another party can dictate what proposals will be considered or ignored, too often producing a nation governed by laws unchecked by meaningful scrutiny or counterargument. Those systems can be changed, too. At the federal level, it is often the voices of legislators who represent tens of millions of voters that are ignored, raising the importance of winning the next election to a point where any behavior can be justified as a necessary means to a beneficial end.

Reducing the power of political parties is only one of the possible actions to lower the level of acrimony that has overtaken American civil life. In almost any endeavor that requires broad citizen participation, it is possible to seek out those systemic features that nudge, or shove, Americans into bitter rival camps. With the stakes so high, civility is an easy habit to jettison. But embracing, even accepting, a continuum of mutual hatred and contempt will cripple this nation.

Civility—the practice of seeking common ground in an atmosphere of mutual respect—is no small thing: it's the key to ensuring America's survival as a champion of common purpose in the service of liberal democracy.

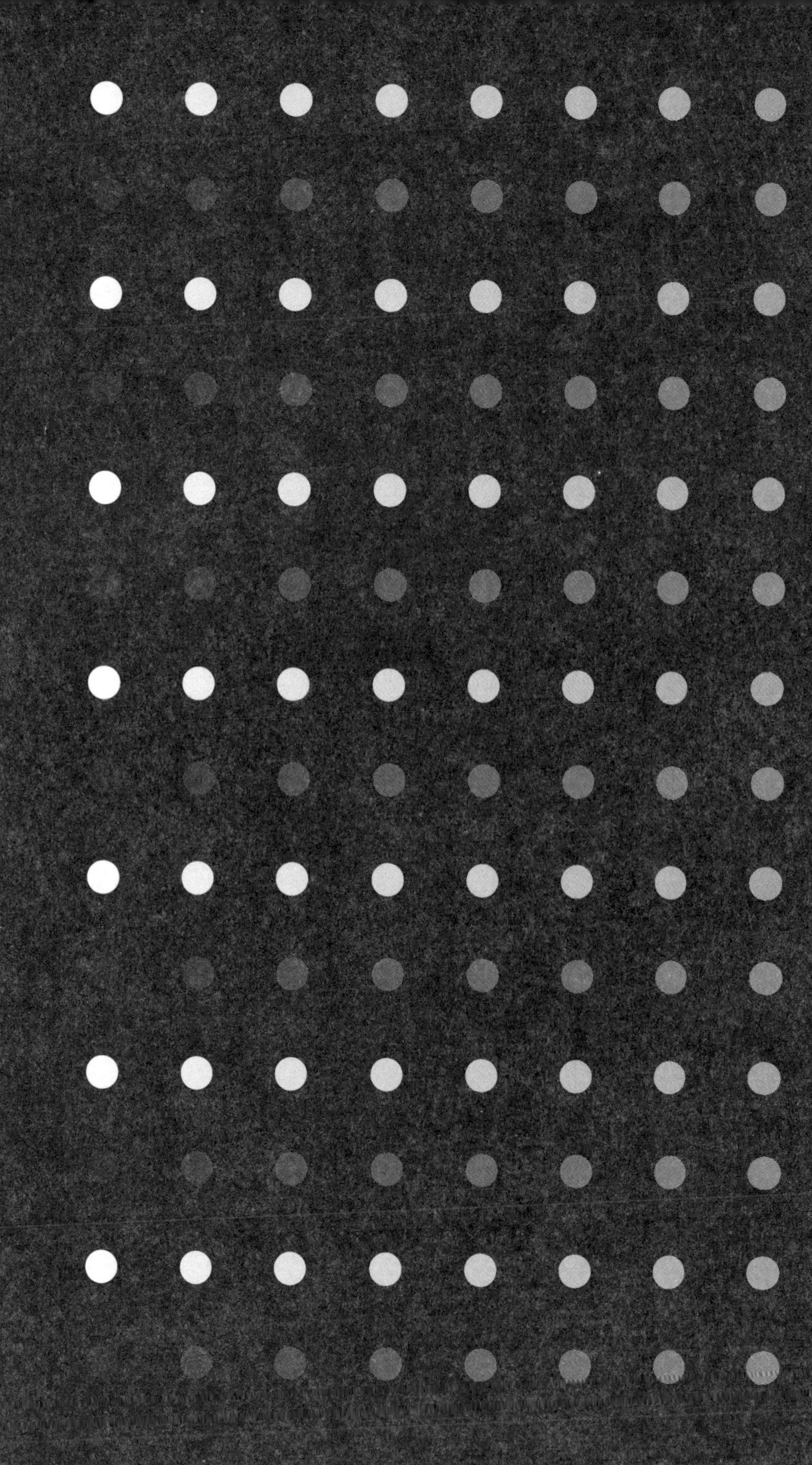

PART III

Social Justice, Civil Disobedience, and Protest

Figure 9.1. Septima Clark teaches a citizenship class in the South Carolina Sea Islands. Standing in the background is Citizenship School teacher Bernice Robinson. Courtesy of SNCC Digital Gateway.

9

On the Meaning of Civility and Citizenship

The Significance of Civil Rights Women Leaders as a Source for Understanding American Democratic Values

KAREN JACKSON-WEAVER

Civility is defined as civilized conduct—especially courtesy or politeness—or a polite act or expression; the recognition of one's common humanity.[1] It is derived from the Latin term *civilitas,* and from *civilis,* which means "relating to citizens." Early use of the term denoted the state of being a citizen and hence good citizenship or orderly behavior. Civility is derived from the word *civis,* which is Latin for "citizen." Citizen is defined as a "native or naturalized person who owes allegiance to a government and is entitled to protection from it," and citizenship means "the status of being a citizen."[2]

As we explore the significance of civility and citizenship in contemporary political contexts, it is important to examine how their meaning has shaped and influenced global political behavior, as well as the systems that promote democratic values and ideals. While interrogating the context of these terms, we must also ask: *Who is the citizen (and who decides who is the citizen)? What are the rights and duties of a citizen? How do we uphold the democratic values and rights of the entire citizenry? What role do individual citizens play in shaping the political landscape to leverage civility, citizenship education, and civic engagement?*

My larger body of research focuses on the role of women as leaders and strategists of the Civil Rights Movement. Throughout American history, many African American women leaders have emphasized the importance of civility and citizenship education because members of the African American community were not treated like citizens or afforded the same rights as other Americans. There is much to learn from their historical work on civic engagement, citizenship education, and leadership development, and the legacy of their commitment to ensure that political institutions and political processes were accessible and equitable for all—and to all.

Septima Clark was the director of education at the Highlander Folk School (HFS) and the director/supervisor of teacher training programs of the Citizenship Education Programs within the Southern Christian Leadership Conference (SCLC) during the civil rights era. In those roles, she served as a key leader and architect of educating others about their rights as citizens of the United States, mostly to empower poor and disenfranchised African Americans in the southern part of the country. Clark developed curricular materials and drew upon her years of teaching to create customized resources. They were instructive, informative, and galvanizing.

Citizenship schools and citizen education programs amplified American democratic values. Clark emphasized that African Americans were citizens and entitled to vote despite widespread illegal practices such as paying poll taxes or passing literacy tests. Citizenship schools and citizen education programs exposed disenfranchised individuals to the full spectrum of rights, liberties, and freedoms afforded to them as American citizens. Clark created a special workbook that included information on the election laws, particularly those setting forth the requirements for registering and voting; laws concerning Social Security; laws relating to taxes; and various other topics of current importance. She went to the school board and obtained information about the duties and functions of the board, as well as meetings dates and attendance policies.

Clark also sought information from the League of Women Voters and other civic groups: "I took this information, which is often couched in sentences and words rather difficult for the grassroots folk to comprehend, and rewrote it in simple, easily comprehensible words. My purpose, of course, was not only to teach them how to read and write but to teach them at the same time things they would have to know in order to start on their way to becoming first class citizens."[3]

Septima Clark did this critical work within an ecosystem of other African American women leaders, including Ella Baker, the first executive director of the Southern Christian Leadership Conference (SCLC) and an advisor to the Student Nonviolent Coordinating Committee (SNCC); Fannie Lou Hamer, the vice chair of the Mississippi Freedom Democratic Party (MFDP) and field secretary of SNCC; and Dorothy Cotton, the director of education with the Southern Christian Leadership Conference. During the 1950s and 1960s, few women held these kinds of leadership roles, especially within organizations traditionally led by African American male clergy members.[4]

Each one of these women worked closely with Reverend Dr. Martin Luther King Jr. While King and other male leaders of the movement have been the subject of numerous books and documentaries, historians and scholars have only begun to study the rich contributions of these women leaders and to examine their significant legacy, especially as it relates to civility, citizenship, and democratic values in American political life.

Historian Bettye Collier-Thomas stresses that in examining women's leadership, we must take a broad approach:

> Rather than focusing on the actions of one individual, sociopolitical analyses examine collectivities and their place in the social environment and political context of their times. Utilizing autobiographical, biographical, statistical, and other types of documentary evidence, these studies attempt to reconstruct historical moments to reveal and assess social, political, and economic changes and continuities. Sociopolitical analyses are extremely important for understanding the contributions of African-American women in the Civil Rights–Black Power Movement, the social changes that took place in American society for African-American women and the dramatic shifts in political consciousness among African-American women and men that became the legacy of future generations.[5]

Baker, Clark, Hamer, and Cotton strived to eradicate segregation and separatist regimes that created social, economic, and political barriers for African Americans because of widespread segregation based on race. They exposed the incivility and inhumane nature of these oppressive conditions by employing a "socio-religious ethical tradition."[6] Their transformative tactics to merge education, religion, and leadership training continued a historical legacy and race-uplift paradigm that became prominent in the post-Reconstruction era. They followed a tradition begun by late 19th-century women such as Charlotte Hawkins Brown, founder of Palmer Memorial Institute, and Nannie Helen Burroughs, founder of the National Training School for Women and Girls, in their quest to empower African Americans at the turn of the twentieth century.[7] They promoted not only literacy and educational opportunities, but also American civic values.

Mary Church Terrell, the first president of the National Association of Colored Women (NACW) and a founder of the National Association for the Advancement of Colored People (NAACP), dedicated her life to eliminating segregation and promoting educational equity. In a speech delivered on October 10, 1906, in Washington, DC, Terrell described the oppressive conditions African Americans often encountered:

> It is impossible for any white person in the United States, no matter how sympathetic and broad, to realize what life would mean to him if his incentive to effort were suddenly snatched away. To the lack of incentive to effort, which is the awful shadow under which we live, may be traced the wreck and ruin of score of colored youth. And surely nowhere in the world do oppression and persecution based solely on the color of the skin appear more hateful and hideous than in the capital of the United States, because the chasm between the principles upon which this Government was founded, in which it still professes to believe, and those which are daily practiced under the protection of the flag, yawn so wide and deep.[8]

The institution-building work that Charlotte Hawkins Brown, Nannie Helen Burrough, and Mary Church Terrell did at the turn of the twentieth century was important because it was holistic in terms of centering education, but this work also underscored the need to address the social, economic, and political disenfranchisement that many in the African American community encountered in early twentieth-century American society. Formerly enslaved men and women continually strived to become literate because they understood that "mastering these skills was an expression of political activism." The skills they gained challenged "the very tenets of slavery itself."[9] Second-class citizenship was not an option.

Reading, writing, and critical thinking provided the intellectual stimulation necessary to question, challenge, and critique their sociopolitical and economic realities.

In 1950, the attorneys for the NAACP made their frontal attack on school segregation as an unconstitutional practice. Four cases were consolidated in the arguments and in the decision: *Brown v. Board of Education of Topeka, Kansas* (the title case of the decision); *Gebhart v. Belton* (from Delaware); *Davis v. County School Board of Prince Edward County, Virginia*; and *Briggs v. Elliot* (from Clarendon County, South Carolina—the home state of Septima Clark).[10]

Cheryl Brown Henderson, the sister of Linda Brown of *Brown v. Board of Education* and daughter of Oliver L. Brown, who was the lead plaintiff in that case, explained that all the children wanted were equal facilities and a chance to become the best they could be, an opportunity to realize their full rights as citizens of the United States. "In many instances schools for African Americans were substandard facilities with outdated textbooks—usually from whites—and often there were no basic supplies. We just wanted equal supplies and facilities. The dedication and competence of our teachers were not the problem; it was the inferior facilities."[11]

African Americans did not lack the talent and insight—they lacked the resources and the means to develop to their fullest potential. Clark became very active in the NAACP's campaign and met with Thurgood Marshall during his visit to South Carolina. Her involvement marked the beginning of her effort to dismantle racist regimes that prohibited African Americans from obtaining equal educational opportunities and full citizenship rights. Clark, Baker, Hamer, and Cotton would devote their lives to promoting equal rights for all disenfranchised Americans.

In an interview, Dorothy Cotton, who worked closely with Septima Clark, recalled:

The Citizenship School Program was the base on which the whole Civil Rights Movement was built. In every area where you can note intense protest—Birmingham, the Mississippi Delta, Southwest Georgia—the people who gave leadership and who gave impetus to local activity had come through the Citizenship School Program. From the beginning, we noticed that the program changed people's view of themselves and their ability to be involved in governing themselves. That is what the program was about. We would go into a community and look for people who had shown some leadership ability—the preachers, the beauticians, the undertakers and others. We'd ask, "Who do you know that's interested in politics, or voter registration?" We tried to find people who had shown some leadership ability, and we invited them to come to the five-day workshops that we were convening at Dorchester Center in Mackintosh, Georgia.[12]

She continued:

The Program brought local leaders and trained them to create "Citizenship Schools" in their local communities. These schools connected voter registration and literacy work to a broad conception of citizenship defined as community problem-solving. The basic primers were documents like the Constitution of the United States, the Declaration of Independence, and scripture. The Citizenship Program was about teaching people to free themselves. One person said it helped black folks to unbrainwash themselves. Blacks in the South had been brainwashed to think they were less than other people, by subtle and not so subtle ways. That was the way the society was structured. I've always been angry about that. People would come to Citizenship Schools and express this anger, get it out, understand that they could learn ways to deal with it. To create something out of that energy. Miss Topsy Eubanks, from

Macon, Georgia, said it another way, after a week of thinking about what it meant to be a citizen: "I feel like I been born again."[13]

Clark also reiterated the importance of the Citizenship Schools:

> There were 897 going from 1957 to 1970. They were in people's kitchens, beauty parlors and all over. Once I heard Andy Young say that the Citizenship Schools were the base on which the whole Civil Rights Movement was built. And that's probably very true because the Citizenship Schools made more people aware of the political situation in their areas. We recruited the wise leaders of their communities like Fannie Lou Hamer in Mississippi. The Citizenship Schools formed the grassroots basis of new statewide political organizations. From one end of the South to the other, if you look at the African American elected officials and the political leaders, you find people who had their first involvement in the training program of the Citizenship Schools.[14]

In 1955, only 25 percent of African Americans in the Deep South were registered to vote. More than 3.5 million were not registered, and many of them were illiterate. In 1962, SCLC joined with the Congress of Racial Equality, the NAACP, the Urban League, and SNCC to form the Voter Education Project. Since Clark, as well as others, had developed the idea of Citizenship Schools between 1957 to 1961, she said "all of the civil rights groups could use our kind of approach because by then we knew it worked." During this period, Clark estimated, 10,000 teachers for Citizenship Schools were trained, and almost 700,000 Blacks registered to vote across the South. Septima Clark worked with other Civil Rights women leaders to create a national network that enabled individuals to become literate and demand their rights as American citizens. By

1970, when she retired from SCLC, more than 2 million more African Americans had voted since 1955.

One cannot address the theme of civility and the commitment to citizenship education without also acknowledging the incivility that came along with this work. Incivility is defined as "the quality or state of being uncivil or a rude or discourteous act."[15] Like many leaders and activists from the Civil Rights Movement era, Clark often encountered varying levels of incivility, including the extreme incivility of physical violence, narrowly escaping from a burning church in Mississippi after a voter registration meeting.

She described the incident in an interview: "We hadn't been out there for five minutes and the whole church was going down." However, they were not deterred. "The next night we had a meeting in the education building of that same church."[16]

Despite the life-threatening situations Clark encountered, she persevered. Today, as we witness more instances of incivility in social media and the public square, ranging from cyberbullying, rudeness, religious intolerance, and blatant discrimination to physical attacks (which were very prevalent during the civil rights era), we must educate others about the tradition of incivility, including violence, in global political discourse and behavior, as well as the contrasting and enduring code of ethics, excellence, and commitment to citizenship education that civil rights women insisted upon for all Americans.

• • •

The legacy of these women has inspired me throughout my career in global higher education. My parents, particularly my mother, instilled within me an ethic of public service—not only for me to lead, but to develop others and their capacity to lead. I have had the good fortune to work in state government under three gubernatorial administrations (McGreevy, Codey, and Corzine) as the inaugural executive director of the New Jersey Amistad

Commission. I am grateful for the vision of the former New Jersey secretary of state, the Reverend Dr. Regena Thomas, and the former commissioner of education, Dr. William Liberera, in supporting me to ensure that all New Jersey schools would teach African American history and integrate it into the larger K–12 social studies curriculum for all children.

The contributions of people of African descent in America have been a missing part of the American historical narrative. Unfortunately, because of recent legislation across the United States, many students are still unaware of women leaders from the Civil Rights Movement and the work they have done to promote civility and citizenship education in American political life.[17] In fact, "since January 2021, 44 states have introduced bills or taken other steps . . . to limit how teachers can discuss racism or sexism" as it relates to the canon of American history.[18]

I transitioned to higher education after my leadership role in state government and have been able to work with students to prepare them for public service at Princeton University's former Woodrow Wilson School of Public and International Affairs (now known as the Princeton School of Public and International Affairs), Harvard University's Kennedy School of Government, and the Blavatnik School of Government at Oxford University. While at Princeton, I taught a myriad of courses, conducted research, and led various university-wide initiatives to highlight the ongoing need for multidimensionality and multifaceted approaches in civic education and leadership development.

From 2014 to 2019, I was able to translate my commitment to global public service in my roles at Harvard's Kennedy School and Oxford University's Blavatnik School of Government. My teaching was done primarily with graduate students, executives, and global leaders on issues related to sociohistorical approaches to public policy, leadership, and governance. At Oxford, I served as the Founding Director of the Executive Public Leaders Program, which is designed for those in leadership within various international governmental ministries, agencies, commissions, or multilateral organizations. My current role at NYU as Senior Associate Vice President of Global Faculty Engagement and Innovation Advancement allows me to work with dynamic institutional partners like Michael DiNiscia and Ellyn Toscano of the Brademas Center's Civility Project and to share critical research on the value of civility in politics and the public square.

Septima Clark, Fannie Lou Hamer, Ella Baker, and Dorothy Cotton are a few historical examples of civil rights women leaders who have made a difference by educating and empowering the citizenry, while insisting upon leveraging civility as a core value toward that end. My hope is that lessons from these civil rights women leaders remind us of the importance of recentering both civility and citizenship education within any political process. Furthermore, they provide us an opportunity to examine our own personal commitment to the values of civility, citizenship education, and civic engagement in public life, while also refining political systems and institutions so that all people in American society may reach their fullest potential.

SELECTED BIBLIOGRAPHY

Bond, Horace Mann. *The Education of the Negro in the American Social Order.* Octagon, 1934.

Brown, Cynthia Stokes. *Ready from Within: Septima Clark and the Civil Rights Movement.* Wild Trees, 1986.

Clark, Septima. *Echo in My Soul.* Dutton, 1962.

Clark, Septima Papers. Avery Research Center, College of Charleston, Charleston, South Carolina.

Collier-Thomas, Bettye, and V. P. Franklin. *My Soul Is a Witness: A Chronology of the Civil Rights Era, 1954–1965.* Henry Holt, 2000.

———. *Sisters in the Struggle: African American Women in the Civil Rights–Black Power Movement.* New York: New York University Press, 2001.

Collins, Patricia Hill. *Black Feminist Thought: Knowledge, Consciousness, and the Politics of Empowerment*. Routledge, 2000.

Cotton, Dorothy. *If Your Back's Not Bent: The Role of the Citizenship Education Program in the Civil Rights Movement*. Atria, 2012.

Crawford, Vicki L., Jacqueline A. Rouse, and Barbara Woods, eds. *Women in the Civil Rights Movement: Trailblazers and Torchbearers*. Carlson, 1990.

Crenshaw, Kimberlé Williams. "King Was a Critical Race Theorist Before There Was a Name for It." *Los Angeles Times*, January 17, 2022. www.latimes.com.

Gates, Henry Louis. "Who's Afraid of Black History?" *New York Times*, February 17, 2023. www.nytimes.com.

Gyant, LaVern, and Deborah Atwater. "Septima Clark's Rhetorical and Ethnic Legacy: Her Message of Citizenship in the Civil Rights Movement." *Journal of Black Studies* (May 26, 1996): 577–92.

Joseph, Peniel E. "Black History Month Exposes the Fallacy of White 'Discomfort.'" CNN, February 2, 2022. www.cnn.com.

Lerner, Gerda. *Black Women in White America*. Pantheon, 1972.

Philip, Mary-Christine. "Then and Now: The Brown Family Still Suing After All These Years." *Black Issues in Higher Education*, January 1994, 32–33.

Riggs, Marcia. *Awake, Arise, and Act: A Womanist Call for Black Liberation*. Pilgrim, 1994.

Schwartz, Sarah. "Where Critical Race Theory Is Under Attack." *Education Week*, June 11, 2021. www.edweek.org.

Terrell, Mary Church. "What It Means to Be Colored in Capital of the United States." Speech delivered October 10, 1906, United Women's Club, Washington, DC.

NOTES

1 *Merriam-Webster's Collegiate Dictionary*, 10th ed. (Merriam-Webster, 1999).

2 *Merriam-Webster's Collegiate Dictionary*.

3 Septima Clark Papers, Box 9, Files 1–29, Avery Research Center, College of Charleston, Charleston, South Carolina.

4 Bettye Collier-Thomas and V. P. Franklin, *Sisters in the Struggle: African-American Women in the Civil Rights and Black Power Movement* (New York University Press, 2001). For more on women leaders and Citizenship Schools in the civil rights era, also see: Septima Clark, *Echo in My Soul* (Dutton, 1962); Dorothy Cotton, *If Your Back's Not Bent: The Role of the Citizenship Education Program in the Civil Rights Movement* (Atria, 2012); Vicki L. Crawford, Jacqueline A. Rouse, and Barbara Woods, eds., *Women in the Civil Rights Movement: Trailblazers and Torchbearers* (Carlson, 1990);

and LaVern Gyant and Deborah Atwater, "Septima Clark's Rhetorical and Ethnic Legacy: Her Message of Citizenship in the Civil Rights Movement," *Journal of Black Studies* (May 26, 1996): 577–92. For more on the Civil Rights Movement generally, see Collier-Thomas and Franklin, *My Soul Is a Witness: A Chronology of the Civil Rights Era, 1954–1965* (Henry Holt, 2000).

5 Collier-Thomas and Franklin, *My Soul Is a Witness*, introduction.

6 Marcia Riggs, *Awake, Arise, and Act: A Womanist Call for Black Liberation* (Pilgrim, 1994), xiv.

7 Riggs, *Awake, Arise, and Act*, 195.

8 Mary Church Terrell, "What It Means to Be Colored in the Capital of the United States" (speech delivered October 10, 1906, United Women's Club, Washington, DC). See also Gerda Lerner, *Black Women in White America* (Pantheon, 1972), 75.

9 Patricia Hill Collins, *Black Feminist Thought: Knowledge, Consciousness, and the Politics of Empowerment* (Routledge, 2000), 147.

10 Horace Mann Bond, *The Education of the Negro in the American Social Order* (Octagon, 1934), 481–83. See also Clark, *Echo in My Soul*, to learn more about her work with the NAACP and other civil rights groups.

11 Mary-Christine Philip, "Then and Now: The Brown Family Still Suing After All These Years," *Black Issues in Higher Education*, January 1994, 32–33.

12 Cynthia Stokes Brown, *Ready from Within: Septima Clark and the Civil Rights Movement* (Wild Trees, 1986), 59–60.

13 Brown, *Ready from Within*.

14 Brown, 70.

15 *Merriam-Webster's Collegiate Dictionary*.

16 Brown, *Ready from Within*, 192.

17 See Kimberlé Williams Crenshaw, "King Was a Critical Race Theorist Before There Was a Name for It," *Los Angeles Times*, Jan 17, 2022; Henry Louis Gates, "Who's Afraid of Black History?," *New York Times*, February 17, 2023; Peniel E. Joseph, "Black History Month Exposes the Fallacy of White 'Discomfort,'" www.cnn.com, February 2, 2022.

18 Sarah Schwartz, "Where Critical Race Theory Is Under Attack," *Education Week*, June 11, 2021 (updated March 23, 2023).

Social Justice and Majority Rule

LARRY COHEN

I grew up in North Philadelphia, and my political activism began as a teenager confronting the brutal racism and repression of the Philadelphia police department and its commissioner, Frank Rizzo. Rizzo went on, as mayor, to lead the Philadelphia Democratic Party from 1972 until 1980. His notion of civility was best expressed when he led a police attack on high school students demonstrating at the Board of Education, shouting, "Get their Black asses," as the cops pulled out their nightsticks, clubbing the students, injuring many, and killing a girl in the process.

This was Philadelphia, Pennsylvania, not Philadelphia, Mississippi.

In politics, civility is first and foremost about the rules. But the point of the rules is not to push decorum or politeness in how we conduct our politics. All too often, such rules are used to stifle dissent, frustrate the will of the public, and enable those who already have power to keep it. In a democracy, civility is about rules that empower majorities while protecting minorities. It is about voting rights and proportionality, so that at every level of society and government, our public life is based on rules that promote majorities while safeguarding the right of dissent for all. Nonviolent forms of assembly, protest, and civil disobedience are pathways for redress of grievances and social change. The rules we live by must defend them.

Seeing police brutality as an adolescent, I learned that the rules matter as much or more than the rulers: without rules that provide majorities with a path for change, the rulers, even when they are elected, matter far less.

I spent most of the last 45 years as an activist, organizer, and elected leader of the Communications Workers of America (CWA), a union representing more than 500,000 workers across North America, including journalists and technicians, tech workers and customer service staff, flight attendants and manufacturing workers. Our union prides itself on rules that protect dissent and promote majority rule—bargaining teams that are elected, contracts that must be ratified by majorities, strikes voted by majorities, leaders at every level elected by majorities—and all voting members count the same.

Civility is critical within the union, since unity does not mean unanimity. Even in a democratic union, there is lots of dissent and sometimes protest, but always nonviolently. The outcome is not at all perfect, but it is civil, and solidarity means a great deal. Solidarity requires tolerance of differing opinions without escalation. Differing opinions are likely on contract proposals and results, but internal union democracy usually mediates disagreements and dissenting views. Arguments can lead to members' quitting, and often to contested elections that can be bitter, but enormous value is placed on ultimate member unity despite these differences.

My own election as national EVP in 1998 was quite divisive, but I immediately reached out to my opponent and discussed how we could work together going forward. Seven years later, when I campaigned for national president, I was elected by acclamation.

Starting in those Rizzo years, I have been arrested for civil disobedience countless times—while battling racism, demonstrating against the Vietnam War, protesting the lack of voting rights, at the White House supporting legalization for immigrants, and often backing strikes and organizing rights for workers.

But in the union, civility has been key, even as we battled for a better life against incredible odds. In my 10 years as president of CWA, I spent much of my time listening to members, often those concerned about or upset with the union. Listening turned out to be much more important than talking, sometimes resulting in new directions.

Civility inside the union is essential, since members have more or less equal power relationships, and majority rule is the norm. But US political decision-making by those in power, and issue campaigns focused on social and economic justice, face inequality and inequity in power and resources in relation to one another. And so, throughout our nation's history, and in my own decades of activism, electoral organizing is often combined with protest, including peaceful but massive demonstrations and civil disobedience. If we think of union decision-making as a guide, much more attention to majority rule in political decision-making would make a difference in both process and outcome.

Social movements focused on national change must mobilize millions of people, ultimately with majority support and the political power needed to govern. And social change occurs only when protest is a path to governance, not an end in itself.

Our challenges as a country are enormous. Twenty million US immigrants have no clear path to citizenship, including 11 million green card holders who are "legal" and permitted to work, but confront huge financial and legal hurdles, incurring significant fees, including for legal support, on the road to citizenship. Millions of American workers are supportive of unions, but most have no path to the bargaining table. We are facing a massive climate crisis, but the national and global response has barely begun to meet the test. The Inflation Reduction Act contains positive incentives for renewable energy, yet these so-called permitting reforms encourage continued new investment in fossil fuels.

Economic inequality in the United States is at record levels, yet the wealth gap continues to increase, and CEOs on average earn 500 times the income of their employees. The United States is retreating rapidly on voting rights, and turnout is at the low end for global democracies. Health care costs are 22 percent of GDP, about twice the average of similar nations, yet health outcomes here are far worse, measured by mortality or access to care.

It's the rules, and not just the rulers! All of the above are rooted in rules that limit participation and, in most cases, prevent majority rule, which would result in policies supported by a majority of Americans. Yet how much attention in our media and beyond is focused on these rules, and the wide disparity between the rules of political engagement in the United States and every other similar democracy? Political engagement—meaning the ability for majorities to govern, including adoption of significant reform—is much harder in the United States than in similar nations, given the need for agreement among the House, Senate, and president compared to parliamentary systems, and, furthermore, the unique role of the federal judiciary to decide on constitutionality and a president not elected by popular vote.

Since January 6, 2021, there has been concern, even by Senate Republicans, about the details of the Electoral College, but almost no focus on amending the constitutional provisions that prevent the majority of the nation from electing the president.

In 2022, when the Senate failed to reenact the Voting Rights Act, it was not because a majority of senators voted the bill down. In fact, since an initial cloture vote failed to receive 60 votes, and a subsequent parliamentary motion to proceed without initial cloture (requiring only 50 votes) also failed, the main motion was never discussed or debated on the Senate floor. The shorthand of filibuster evokes the bygone era of *Mr. Smith Goes to Washington,* when a senator takes the floor and holds it for as long as she or he can talk, preventing a vote on a bill or resolution until her or his colleagues give up and agree to move on to other Senate business.

Neither Democratic senators, nor, again, the news media have explained to the public that for the last 40 years we have not had a filibuster. Instead, we have a procedure known as initial cloture, requiring 60 votes to move a motion to the floor for debate and discussion—which means that all 60 senators who support having debate and a vote on a piece of legislation must be present on the floor to vote for cloture, with final passage requiring only a majority of senators, not all 60. However, the rule does not require the 41 (or more) senators opposed to cloture to be on the floor in order to block it.

In another twist, when reenactment of voting rights was under consideration, there was an attempt to carve out an exception from the cloture rule by a motion either to exempt civil rights and voting bills from the 60-vote threshold or to implement a "talking filibuster," which failed to get the 50 votes required to change Senate procedure. Ironically, a simple majority of the Senate could have changed procedure and bypassed the 60-vote requirement for cloture.

Senate procedures defy logic and certainly defy majority rule, but, more importantly, block nearly every attempt to legislate economic and social change on a national level.

Rightly so, when Amazon workers in Staten Island voted to organize their workplace in 2022, many in the media cheered the breakthrough! As Starbucks workers continue to win representation elections at more than 150 stores, again: great reporting by the media. Yet rules that allow endless employer delays and make negotiations for a first contract all but impossible receive almost no attention.

Amazon and Starbucks management have decided that endless delay with $1,000-an-hour legal bills is well worth the cost. The federal judiciary and the National Labor Relations Board procedures all encourage management delay. Again, in nearly every other democracy, the outcomes of bargaining might be in doubt, but not the very existence of a contract. There is no finality in the United States to first-contract negotiations, despite repeated passage by the House and support by majorities in the Senate of bills guaranteeing this right in 2009 and again in 2021.

To amend rules grounded in the Constitution is a tortuous process, with no provision for a national referendum based on majority rule. The federal judiciary, now controlled by conservatives, operates in many ways like a third legislative branch, but to change the Supreme Court especially, it is again subject to federal legislation and the obstacle of Senate rules.

In a series of cases, the federal judiciary has ruled that money equals speech, so record wealth disparities translate into barriers to political change. 2022 saw record spending in primary elections, much of it dark money, hiding the donors and spent primarily on negative media. Again, the rules are the deterrent to democracy—in this case, state and national party rules.

Why all the media and voter focus on the candidates, or rulers, versus the rules that seem to be controlling the outcome? Why does candidate infatuation, if not addiction, occupy media and voter attention, when for those of us committed to social change, the rules seem to prevent that change? Our best opportunity is to build coalitions of issue-based groups that connect the rules that must change to their issue campaigns.

Candidates in the United States are very much on their own, not accountable to a party or political organization and more exposed to personal attacks from their opponents, rather than vulnerable because of political differences. I have worked closely with many candidates on the left in the Democratic Party. But at the end of the day, those candidates and their staff are responsible for success or failure, certainly not a political party or organization. In other democracies, there is much more accountability of candidates and elected representatives. Political organization in addition to voting can provide more focus on issues.

Many, if not most, leaders of social change organizations, at least in private, bemoan the state of the Democratic Party and consider the current Republican Party a right-wing authoritarian organization with little use for democracy. Yet our party rules, including the Electoral College, all but prevent new parties from being relevant. It would seem that social change activists should focus at least some attention on changing the state and national party organizations that control the candidate nomination process and voting rules for primaries. Yet very few organizations even begin to do that. The Unity Reform Commission of the Democratic Party, established by the 2016 National Convention, did succeed in limiting the role of nonelected delegates in the presidential nominating process. At least 10 state parties, mostly Western, have elected reform leaders who are changing the party in their own states. And about 60 Democratic National Committee members have formed a reform group focused in part on dark money in the primaries.

Obviously, despite the rules, social change in our nation has been possible. The New Deal, civil rights, Medicare, and the Affordable Care Act are all examples of significant national political change within the system.

Today, social justice movements need a combination of mass organizing; protest, including civil disobedience; and electoral and political action. Mass organizing, as with union organizing, requires internal civility, treating participants with equal respect, and listening more than talking. Protest similarly requires civility internally and externally, or the message is obscured. Nonviolence in thought as well as action is an essential element of civil disobedience.

In my own experience, civil disobedience training has preceded every action. Whether blocking streets, occupying offices, sitting in at the White House or Capitol, or even standing in picket lines blocking trucks, practicing silence and avoiding resisting arrest have been crucial elements to success. Nonviolence and verbal civility are critical elements in effective civil disobedience.

Yet the right wing in our nation has abandoned civility, along with democracy. There is no pretense by Republicans to majority rule or tolerance of opponents. Indeed, a growing rejoinder among GOP politicians is that the United States is a republic and not a democracy. In fact, opponents, including voters, are demonized—and vulgar banners and appeals to violence about Biden and Biden voters are not uncommon.

At times, the debate around civility may seem antiquated. After the January 6 attack on the Capitol, much of the conversation has focused on the illegal actions of the insurrectionists, and rightly so. But our failure to stay focused on the need for social change and the path forward might also be contributing to the rise of authoritarianism, as working-class Americans abandon hope. The majority of American workers have seen their living standards stagnate for decades. Trump and his threats are not sufficient to mobilize a massive grassroots movement for social change.

For young workers facing seemingly unending barriers to happiness, we cannot simply talk about the right-wing threat. For Black Americans still reliving the consequences of slavery, abandonment of Reconstruction, and segregation, we cannot ignore social justice. For millions of Americans unable to improve their conditions at work through collective bargaining, we cannot simply put off a living wage or meaningful collective bargaining rights.

We can't hide from the climate crisis by taking baby steps toward sustainability, as fires and floods spread. We can't pretend we have equal opportunity, while billionaires control election spending and the wealth gap explodes, even during the COVID pandemic.

The defense of civility as a necessary condition for a functioning democracy must be linked to real change and significant movement toward majority rule. Our political life cannot be about only candidates and their elections, instead of policy results that follow voting results.

First steps include: ending the Senate filibuster and adopting universal voting rights; passing legislation limiting the ever-expanding role of the federal judiciary and considering term limits for judges; limiting dark money in primaries, which the party controls, and then legislating campaign finance reform for general elections as soon as possible; and adopting simple economic justice measures that are nearly universal outside the US, including providing health care and long-term care, early childhood and higher education, so that there is a basis for equal opportunity.

Civility rests on rules that are fair and a life that is at least decent for all. It's OK if we argue and disagree, but we must create a deep and universal feeling that this is our world and change is possible.

In Defense of Incivility

CHARLTON MCILWAIN

Civility is for suckers. That was my immediate reaction to being asked to speak on a panel about civility.[1] The panel was typical: four people occupying our own little square on a Zoom screen, offering thoughts and conversing with each other about the role of civility in today's politics. Perhaps my knee-jerk reaction was a bit too solipsistic. Given my audience, the occasion, and the suggestion that my talk might even model the topic itself, I briefly reconsidered. Briefly.

Is Civility Even Real?

It has been a foregone conclusion to me for some time that the concept of civility is dying, if not already long dead. And this is as it should be. Defined and used today, civility is a set of norms and conventions that prescribe the proper way to engage in public discourse. Politeness. Mutual respect. Seeing the world from another's perspective. Listening. Decorum. Disagreeing with grace and a smile. These elements have long been among the hallmarks of civility. But the truth of the matter is that none of them define what is possible or promoted in our current social, political, and media environment. None describe what takes place in town halls across the United States, where rants about the evils of critical race theory run rampant. None of these components reflect the words of recalcitrant politicians whose only response to one tragic school shooting after another is "thoughts and prayers." None describe the apathy surrounding a White legislator who questions two of her Black colleagues' (both natural and naturalized citizens) patriotism, saying they should "go back to the Middle East." These norms of civility are certainly not in play when a head of state would be cheered, not sanctioned, for calling Haiti a "shithole country," or when that same crowd would chuckle and applaud a political rally speaker who called a whole group of fellow Americans "garbage."

And so we must come to grips with the reality that for all intents and purposes, civility is dead. In fact, I dare say that for most of the world who is not White, or male, or Christian, civility has always been a useful illusion. I say civility is for suckers because both our present and our past history about social change, about protest, about mass political action demonstrate to us time and again that civility is simply the card that those in power play when masses of people threaten that power.

A hollow notion of civility is what gave us such bankrupt policies as a fairness doctrine (resurrected in our current networked news and opinion environment), which once suggested that every viewpoint, every voice, every rant, screed, or diatribe of mis- or disinformation should be heard, distributed, engaged, and reckoned with.

When we move from the domain of speech to the domain of collective action and social change, we find that notions of civility once birthed a related notion of civil disobedience—a conundrum and contradiction that only those wielding state power have the straight face to articulate and enforce. Historically, when your collective action poses a real threat, those who have power refer to it as a "civil disorder" and respond by trying to set you straight, bring you in line, manufacture your consent, your obedience, your subservience. Yes, your speech is free, but so long as it is spoken within the confines of civil procedure, it will buy you nothing in the way of changing the status quo, shifting power, or giving the historically disenfranchised greater access to it.

I know that thus far these claims may sound like a collection of non sequiturs. But I make these seemingly disconnected points to advance a specific argument about why civility serves the status quo and how incivility—a challenge to a fundamental deficiency of civility—more strongly facilitates social change by shifting power.

Before describing what that deficiency is, I want to offer the observation that the state and those with access to power only respond to and consider social change when individuals and/or the masses resist civility. To put it more clearly, if civility is the tool that those in power deploy to maintain their power, then it is incivility—not civility—that drives social change.

Incivility and Racial Justice Activism

Now I want to speak about civility and social change in the context of racial justice activism. More specifically, I want to say a few words about it in the context of the Black Lives Matter movement, the movement for Black lives, the collective efforts to seek and attain justice for people and communities of color.

Before I proceed, let's take a moment to look at the movement's success. Not since the late 1960s has the issue of race writ large, or issues of racial injustice in the criminal justice system, been on the list of US citizens' top concerns until the year and years following the articulation of BLM as a concept, a rallying cry for collective action, an organization, and a set of policy prescriptions. These issues have stayed atop the public agenda in a more sustained way than any of the high-profile racial issues that plagued us in the 1970s, '80s, '90s, and the early 2000s.

In the years that I focused on BLM activists and activism, I was struck by their strident desire to separate themselves from previous generations of civil rights leaders. Why did they do this? Because they rightly recognized that their parents' and grandparents' civil rights revolution was framed by civility. They recognized that it was mired in respectability politics and propelled by the notion of playing by the rules as dictated by those who were willing to bend them only so far, mired in patriarchal notions of hierarchy and power that built and sustained white supremacy. Sure, they achieved some gains, some very important gains—such as the Voting Rights Act. The Fair Housing Act. An end to formalized segregation and Jim Crow. Increased but still inadequate racial representation in Congress, and in state and local governments. But the civil rights revolution didn't get us enough to prevent that same system of power and the same people who have wielded that power from continuing to discriminate against Black and Brown people in education, and employment, and housing, and economic opportunity—or from policing and criminalizing our communities at every turn. And so the generation that coined cancel culture took hold of all that BLM stood for and were successful because they were so relentless in their incivility.

Who can forget the BLM activists who stormed the stages of presidential candidates from Hillary Clinton and Bernie Sanders to Mitt Romney and Donald Trump to demand that they be listened to, to demand that those candidates say the words "Black Lives Matter," to demand recognition of the persistent violence that our criminal justice system perpetuates against communities of color?

And who can forget the results that followed—more articulated words in the 2016 Democratic Party platform than were ever before articulated. Same for the Republican Party, but to a comparatively lesser degree. And more articulated specific policy proposals to address issues of police violence and systemic racism than we have seen in recent decades.

Who can forget the many images, in Ferguson, in Baltimore, in New York, in Oakland, and in Los Angeles, and Chicago, and Atlanta, and Charlotte, and Washington, DC, where BLM activists stood defiantly—hurling epithets and speaking truths about law enforcement complicity in sustaining racial violence—in front of thick blue walls of cops armed with the latest military machinery, prepared to do what it took to keep the protests civil and in order.

BLM was powerful and successful because it leveraged the juxtapositions of state brutality and so-called citizen incivility through the millions of memes and mashups, images of cold, dead Black and Brown bodies alongside those who marched out of line, out of step, and out of order, beyond the boundaries of police-sanctioned protest routes. Protesters were successful because they used their voices and their cameras and their phones and their social media feeds in uncivil ways to capture, distribute, and castigate the actions of police and politicians who insist that BLM's act to render transparency is an affront to the privacy of government actors who sustain their power by working and lurking in the shadows.

And, so, where do we draw the line for the acceptable level of incivility that propels a collective assault against entrenched power? Violence is deplorable and certainly must be one of those lines. But perhaps we should draw the line at the point where those in power are the ones who are expected to and who actually live up to their ideals of civility towards the masses—a type of civility that compels those in power to truly recognize us, to truly understand our position, to respectfully address us, hear our voices, and shift, relinquish, or share access to power, privilege, opportunity, and freedom.

The Immorality of Civility, Circa 2016, 2024

When Donald Trump was first elected president in 2016, I wrote the following words in a CNN op-ed:

> The narrative supporting the "new white" wants us to accept four primary truths. The left's identity politics are too divisive. Liberal elites are too insular. Class—not race—anxieties animate today's white working-class frustration and fears. Finally, whether Trump maintains the new order, or the left overthrows it, we must invest our time and energy in understanding white people. As much as this narrative might argue otherwise, however, the new white is the old white under different cover. If we allow their pleas to heap more attention on white America, black and brown Americans will find ourselves refighting the battles our civil rights forebears fought, rather than continuing our long march toward racial justice.[2]

Trump won the presidency again in 2024. And again, the national narrative calls for introspection in much the same way. But it is the fact that Americans once again elected Trump that exposes the farce and folly of continued insistence that civility should rule democratic politics and the quest for social change and justice. Power now resides in the hands of those whose actions of the past almost-decade have normalized and sanctioned state and public vulgarity and violence. Those of us who cling to our petty and petulant racial identity politics have been bullied into submission, to accept once again in the most blatant and explicit ways possible that not only does power reign supreme, but White Power reigns supreme.

This civility as a concept has no moral center, because it compels subservience to those who have and refuse to cede power. And civility without power is simply acquiescence. Civility is morally bankrupt because it compels us to kowtow to those who deny our very humanity. It's the proverbial house Negro. It is the Black and Brown sidekick of Hollywood history, who must already be subservient to and heap praise on his White hero or savior. It is what compels a president to say that "there are good people on both sides," when those on one of the sides are torch-bearing, Confederate-flag-waving, white supremacists, neo-Nazis, and Ku Klux Klan members. It is the knee-jerk response to go high when those in power go low.

If we are to ever get on a path to something different, civility cannot be our guide. It cannot be the principle that determines our tactics. For those of us fighting to change society in a way that lives up to our still-theoretical ideals of equality, incivility must animate our marching orders. We must act not in accordance with power and those who exercise it. We must compel those in power to see us, to recognize us, to engage and contend with us and our interests. We must act in uncivil ways that demand recognition of our humanity and our right to participate in, benefit from, and share legitimate control of the levers of democracy and its institutions.

NOTES

1 "Civility: Social Justice, Civil Disobedience, and Protest," organized by the John Brademas Center of New York University, June 1, 2022, www.nyu.edu.

2 Charlton McIlwain, "The New White Is the Same Old Story," CNN, December 21, 2016, www.cnn.com.

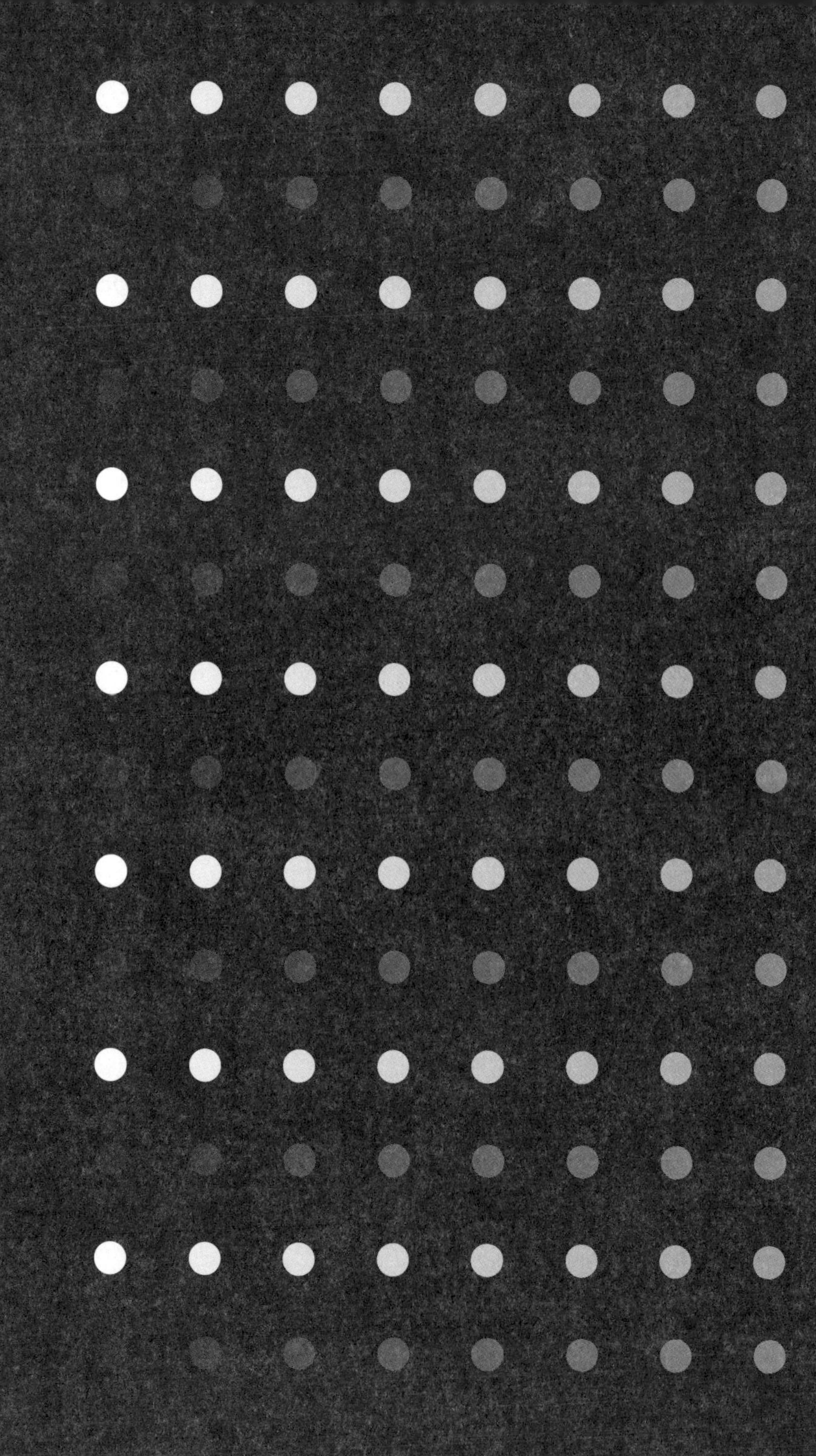

PART IV

In News Media and Social Media

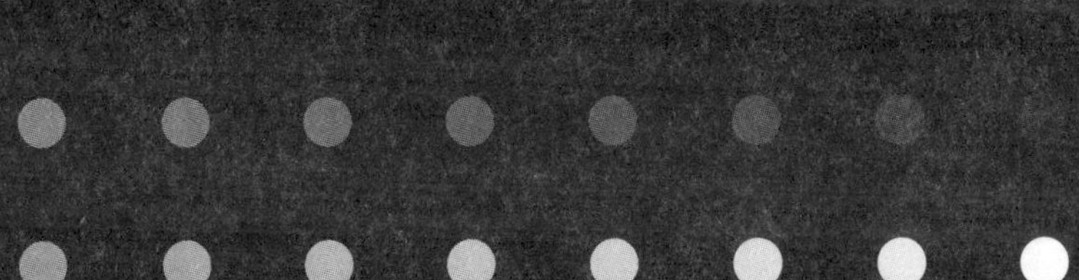
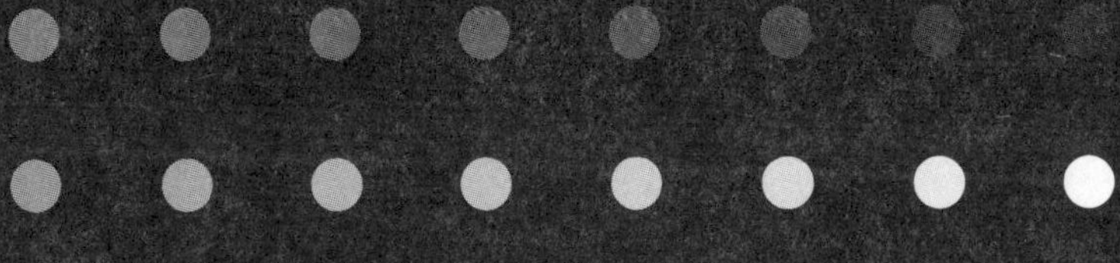
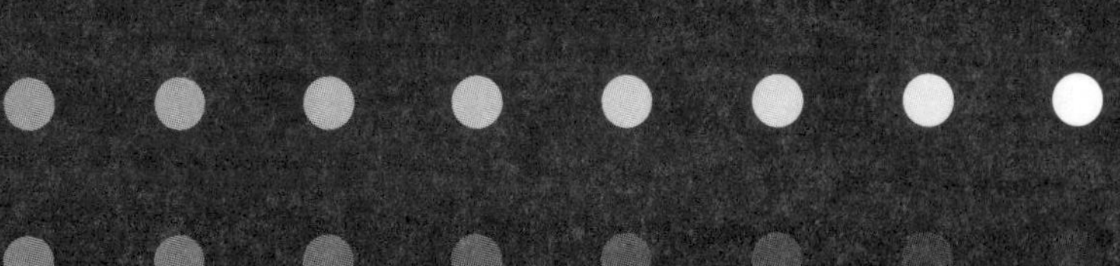

Deceptive Distrust and Democratic Institutions

SARAH SOBIERAJ

I have spent 15 years researching extreme political incivility in the United States and highlighting the potential consequences of its toxicity. Even so, I was not fully prepared to see the news that emerged from the January 6 attack on the US Capitol: images of rioters scaling the building, legislators crouching for cover in the Senate chamber, frightened staffers barricading themselves into offices, debris and glass shards from shattered windows strewn in the halls. The chaos and sense of vulnerability exceeded my imaginings.

The participants were trying to stop the election from being certified because they believed they were defending democracy from an illegitimate seizure of power. The election had been stolen. Their insurrection, cast as a patriotic act by the sitting president, was uncivil, illegal, frightening, and violent. And although the attack was unprecedented, the participants' indignation calls to mind a broader phenomenon: an ideologically selective, deep distrust of core democratic intuitions and processes on the grounds that they are irreparably biased.

Ideologically selective political distrust can be found in beliefs about journalism on the right and the Supreme Court on the left.[1] We also see ideologically selective distrust in other social institutions, such as policing, higher education, and science, all of which are political, if in a more abstract sense. Institutional distrust, including that which falls along party lines, may be justified. But false narratives of illegitimacy that distort, mislead, and breed unwarranted distrust—such as those about the "stolen" 2020 election—merit our attention.

Whether or not the January 6 violence was incited by former President Trump, the participants' beliefs about the stolen election fall largely on his shoulders. Trump made repeated public assertions that the election had been "rigged" by the Democrats and claimed that they used "massive" voting fraud to steal the election.[2] His accusations were echoed by a subset of vocal party members (e.g., Ted Cruz, Kevin McCarthy, Steve Scalise), given additional air by sympathetic media personalities (e.g., Maria Bartiromo, Chris Salcedo, Tucker Carlson), embraced by Christian nationalists, and amplified via social media.[3]

The claims were unfounded. They have been dismissed by several judges, state election officials, and the Department of Homeland Security's Office of Intelligence and Analysis. Over a month *prior* to the January 6 attack, Attorney General William Barr released a statement indicating that the Department of Justice investigation found no evidence of widespread election fraud.[4] Regardless, the former president maintained—and continues to share—his insistence upon the illegitimacy of the 2020 election and his support for the insurrectionists. During his 2024 presidential campaign, he described the rioters as "unbelievable patriots" and referred to those in prison for their involvement as "hostages."[5]

In contrast to accounts of declining governmental trust in the United States as emerging organically in response to changes in the sociopolitical context (e.g., economic changes, social changes, etc.), Amy Fried and Douglas Harris argue that distrust has been strategically manipulated by political elites for political gain.[6] Their history of conservative anti-government campaigns in the United States argues that since at least the 1920s, the conservative wing of the Republican party has successfully mobilized distrust to support and undermine proposed policies, fund and strengthen political organizations and movements, influence voters and election outcomes, and amass power in the parts of the national government under their control.

My interest here is in thinking about a special breed of distrust work: politically motivated distrust claims about *democratic institutions or processes* that are grounded in *disinformation*—such as those made about the 2020 election.[7] Fried and Harris have shown that weaponized distrust can shape election outcomes; we need a way to recognize and talk about strategic political speech in which the outcome is not an unwarranted loss of faith in a *candidate*, but an unwarranted loss of faith in *elections*.[8] Even so, the conceptual work feels fraught. I have observations and ideas, but also worries and questions. I present them here and invite others to advance the discussion.

Observations

Political communication provides several related concepts that are useful in helping identify efforts to manufacture and weaponize deceptive democratic distrust—particularly concepts related to strategic rhetoric such as disinformation, propaganda, and outrage, which offer us purchase but fall short of capturing the radiating impact of this rhetoric. While it is beyond the scope of this essay to provide thorough conceptual maps for each of them, I sketch their contributions below.

DISINFORMATION is "a rhetorical strategy that produces and disseminates false or misleading information in a deliberate effort to confuse, influence, harm, mobilize, or demobilize a target audience."[9] Dangerous distrust can also emerge from other kinds of information. Speakers can cherry-pick accurate statistics to create a picture that is misrepresentative, using what Wardle and Derakhshan classify as malinformation.[10] Alternatively, they might share deeply believed pieces of information that are false (misinformation). I specify disinformation to narrow our focus, isolating communication that erodes trust in institutions and processes via the strategic use of false or knowingly unsubstantiated information.[11]

Distrust claims made against political institutions and processes generally implicate multiple people or entire organizations, making CONSPIRACY THEORIES relevant. Conspiracy theories involve "attempts to explain the ultimate causes of significant social and political events and circumstances with claims of secret plots by two or more powerful actors."[12] Conceptually, this helps train our lens on claims involving collusion as well as deceit and malfeasance. It also reminds us to exclude distrust claims linked to efficiency or efficacy, which are common but usually imply ineptness rather than malevolence. Importantly, because claims of collusion and conspiracy *may be correct*, conspiracy claims become relevant to unmerited institutional distrust when paired with disinformation.

Disinformation and conspiracy theories are tools in the attention-seeking repertoire Jeff Berry and I have referred to as OUTRAGE.[13] Outrage is a genre of political media and its characteristic mode of communication, which involves political speech intended to provoke an emotional response (e.g., fear, anger, and moral indignation) from the audience in the interest of ratings, votes, clicks, donations, etc. Purveyors of outrage draw on many different tools, including disinformation and conspiratorial explanation, but also personal attack, misrepresentative exaggeration, mockery, sensationalism, and forecasts of impending doom. In thinking about the tactical fomentation of distrust, outrage reminds us to consider not only accuracy and intent, but also the provocation of emotion and the pursuit of "profit," broadly defined.

These three concepts (disinformation, conspiracy theory, and outrage) help us imagine how attempts to manufacture distrust might look and sound, but they center on speakers (disinformation, outrage) and content (disinformation, conspiracy theory, outrage). They do not explore reception. DEFAMATION starts to open that door. There are varied legal definitions of defamation, but at its core, it involves making false statements about a person that damage their reputation and, in so doing, cause harm. While discussions of defamation are far more common in legal discourse than in political communication literature, attention to the way false claims are received—that is, to outcomes—inches us toward the bigger issues at play in studying trust in democratic institutions.

When the harm is more diffuse, HATE SPEECH—although multidimensional and contested—becomes instructive. Hate speech targets a group or a person as a member of a group. Precisely *which* groups varies across the myriad definitions, but the focal concern is with those who are or have been historically marginalized, for whom hatred may be particularly dangerous. Other common criteria appear in definitions of hate speech crafted by lawmakers, academics, and digital platforms, including but not limited to: presence of hateful content, ability to incite hatred or violence, and intent to harm.[14] Although hate speech is centrally concerned with disadvantage (not what comes to mind when we think about Congress, whose members have power), its attention to rhetoric with the potential to harm an entire community has great relevance to attempts to manufacture unmerited distrust in the institutions that support democracy.[15]

Ideas

Drawing upon these concepts in the context of the election narratives that circulated in 2020 and 2021, we might tentatively identify deceptive democratic distrust as speech that: (1) targets an institution or a person or a group of people working in (or with) an institution in their role as representatives of that institution (target); (2) strives to create or increase public distrust in the institution or the group of people working in (or with) the institution in the service of political, professional, or personal advantage (goal); (3) presents real and alleged institutional problems as the result of malfeasant and/or deceitful politically motivated behavior (frame) (4) on the basis of information that is known to be inaccurate, misrepresentative, grossly exaggerated, or unsubstantiated (claims), (5) using appeals to emotion, especially anger, fear, disgust, and righteousness (style).

Drawing inductively from transcripts and news accounts capturing the election-related remarks made by Donald Trump, supportive lawmakers, and news personalities brings some recurring themes to the fore. First, there is a tendency to minimize complexity, uncertainty, and ambiguity in favor of certainty. Second, relatively minor missteps or problems are proffered as conflagratory evidence that the 2020 election as a whole was faulty. Third, in claims making, little evidence is provided beyond the speakers' assertion of behind-the-curtain knowledge, even in instances where access and direct experience appear absent. Fourth, disconfirming results of investigatory reports are often presented as further evidence of corruption or bias; rather than allaying fears, they confirm them. Finally, purveyors of deceptive distrust frequently construct caricatured in-groups (heroic) and out-groups (villainous) as central elements of their narratives.

These attributes are derived from anecdotal evidence that may be unrepresentative. Still, I offer them as a possible starting point for empirical research on efforts to manufacture distrust.

Worries

What would it mean to bring a critical lens to distrust claims, when distrust is an essential element of democracy?[16] Distrust is deliberately institutionalized in constitutional democracies—"baked in" to legitimate democratic systems.[17] In the US case, for example, checks and balances were designed to mitigate abuse of power, and elections hold representatives accountable to those they serve. Oversight bodies and processes exist because it is assumed that some office holders may break rules, behave unethically, or prove incompetent. Freedom of the press, freedom of speech, and freedom of assembly are testaments to the perceived importance of public monitoring and criticism to protect the citizenry from those in government who would prefer that their indiscretions stay hidden. Accordingly, Norris cautions against overly romantic views of trust: blind faith in political institutions may make the citizenry overly compliant; "skeptical trust," in contrast, is appropriate and healthy.

Would the benefit of being able to identify illegitimate distrust claims outweigh the risk of overreach? Claims of institutional illegitimacy are not categorically inaccurate, and some are of great import. Given our current political climate, concepts and criteria designed to identify unfounded distrust-mongering are almost certain to be used to discredit valid efforts to bring attention to wrongdoings, process failures, etc. Journalistic errors happen, but "fake news" has been used to cast doubt on high-quality news work and to denigrate both news organizations and journalists. How many legitimate calls for action and accountability might be discounted or explained away as disingenuous once we code some expressions of distrust as courageous/virtuous and others as deceptive/malignant?

If distrust claims are deemed dangerous, would they be silenced? While we would not expect government intervention, given the protections provided by the First Amendment, social media platforms have greater leeway. Cognizance of social media platforms' right to decide what violates their terms of service means recognizing that platform concerns about *deceptive* distrust could pave the way for the censoring of legitimate content regarding political corruption, efficacy, and impropriety. What's more, the arbiters of acceptability would not be subject to public oversight.

In light of the complexities related to this breed of incivility, input from other scholars concerned about the political climate and information environment in the United States is especially important. My hope is that together we can develop the tools we need to recognize and interrogate attempts to manufacture institutional distrust, as such weaponization efforts have proven electorally expedient and are likely to continue.

NOTES

1 See Megan Brenan, "Americans' Trust in Media Remains Near Record Low," Gallup News, October 18, 2022, news.gallup.com; Claire Brockway and Bradley Jones, "Partisan Gap Widens in Views of the Supreme Court," Pew Research Center, August 7, 2019, www.pewresearch.org; Joseph Copeland, "Favorable Views of Supreme Court Remain Near Historic Low," Pew Research Center, August 9, 2024, www.pewresearch.org; and Jeffrey Gottfried and Jacob Liedke, "Partisan Divides in Media Trust Widen, Driven by a Decline Among Republicans," MediaWell, August 31, 2021, mediawell.ssrc.org.

2 To review the election-related claims made by President Trump prior to January 6, 2021, I recommend his recorded statement from December 2020, originally posted by the White House Facebook account. The video and transcript are available on CSPAN, www.c-span.org.

3 See Tucker Carlson, "Yes, the Election was Rigged for Joe Biden. Here's How," Fox News, November 23, 2020, www.foxnews.com; Sheera Frenkel, "How Misinformation 'Superspreaders' Seed False Election Theories," *New York Times*, November 23, 2020, www.nytimes.com; Jack Jenkins, "Faith Leaders Ask Why Jan. 6 Report Left Out Christian Nationalism," *Washington Post*, December 29, 2022, www.washingtonpost.com; and Manu Raju and Jeremy Herb, "House Conservatives Urge Trump Not to

Concede and Press for Floor Fight over Election Loss," CNN, December 7, 2020, www.cnn.com.

4 Evan Perez and Devan Cole, "William Barr Says There Is No Evidence of Widespread Fraud in Presidential Election," CNN, December 1, 2020, www.cnn.com.

5 Lisa Mascaro, Mary Clare Jalonick, and Jill Colvin, "Trump Is Making the Jan. 6 Attack a Cornerstone of His Bid for the White House," Associated Press, March 19, 2024, apnews.com.

6 Amy Fried and Douglas B. Harris, *At War with Government: How Conservatives Weaponized Distrust from Goldwater to Trump* (Columbia University Press, 2021).

7 My interest in attempts to manufacture institutional distrust does not rely on our trust levels being at an all-time low. I make no claims in this regard. There are many who already do wonderful work on political trust and distrust over time, as well as research that documents institutional trust in various ways. Admittedly, there is room for richer understanding; see Jack Citrin and Laura Stoker, "Political Trust in a Cynical Age," *Annual Review of Political Science* 21, no. 1 (2018): 49–70, for a discussion of the limits presented by the available survey data most frequently used to address these topics.

8 I am fearful about the possible implications of unwarranted distrust in democratic institutions: widespread distrust might promote cynicism, feelings of inefficacy, disengagement, political destabilization, or even acts of aggression or violence. But whether it does, for whom, and under what circumstances are empirical questions for future research, rather than something I take for granted.

9 Samuel Spies, "Defining Disinformation," MediaWell, October 22, 2019, mediawell.ssrc.org.

10 Claire Wardle and Hossein Derakhshan, *Information Disorder: Toward an Interdisciplinary Framework for Research and Policymaking* (Council of Europe, 2017).

11 In thinking about concrete organizations, institutions, and processes, I find disinformation a more analytically useful term than propaganda. As understood by philosopher Jason Stanley in *How Propaganda Works* (Princeton University Press, 2015), propaganda may be sincere and based on accurate information; its distinguishing feature is that its political purpose is to support or undermine *ideals* (e.g., freedom, equality).

12 Karen M. Douglas, Joseph E. Uscinski, Robbie M. Sutton, Aleksandra Cichocka, Turkay Nefes, Chee Siang Ang, and Farzin Deravi, "Understanding Conspiracy Theories," *Political Psychology* 40 (2019): 3–35.

13 Sarah Sobieraj and Jeffrey M. Berry, "From Incivility to Outrage: Political Discourse in Blogs, Talk Radio, and Cable News," *Political Communication* 28, no. 1 (2011): 19–41; and Jeffrey M. Berry and Sarah Sobieraj, *The Outrage Industry: Political Opinion Media and the New Incivility* (Oxford University Press, 2014).

14 Andrew Sellars, "Defining Hate Speech," *Berkman Klein Center Research Publication* (2016): 25–30.

15 As do subsets of hate speech such as DANGEROUS SPEECH, which Susan Benesch defines as "any form of expression (e.g., speech, text, or images) that can increase the risk that its audience will condone or commit violence against members of another group." Dangerous Speech Project, "Dangerous Speech: A Practical Guide," www.dangerousspeech.org.

16 See Pippa Norris, *In Praise of Skepticism: Trust but Verify* (Oxford University Press, 2022); and Mark Warren, "Trust and Democracy," *The Oxford Handbook of Social and Political Trust* (Oxford University Press, 2018), 75–94.

17 See John Braithwaite, "Institutionalizing Distrust, Enculturating Trust," *Trust and Governance* 343 (1998): 356; and Piotr Sztompka, "Trust, Distrust, and Two Paradoxes of Democracy," *European Journal of Social Theory* 1 (1998): 19–32.

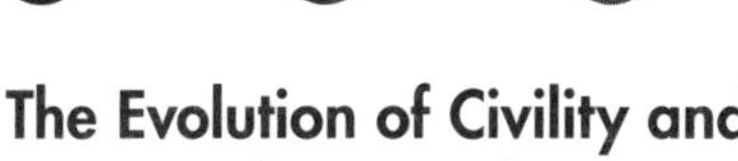

The Evolution of Civility and News in the Digital Age

PAUL CHEUNG

Civility in public discourse is a complex issue, especially for communities of color who have historically been labeled "uncivilized." The term has been weaponized in a paradoxical manner by Western culture. It is used as a justification for exclusion, barring access to spaces and opportunities, while simultaneously imposing Western standards of civility, demanding adherence to its norms. This situation creates conditional inclusion for those communities who adopt Western values and norms, gaining limited acceptance, while allowing Western culture to maintain its dominance by setting the terms of both exclusion and conditional acceptance.

The historical portrayal of Indigenous people in America as lacking "civilized" qualities was used to justify their displacement from lands and resources.[1] Similarly, depictions of Black people as "uncivilized" served to dehumanize and exclude them from education, employment, and public spaces dominated by White society. Stereotypical portrayals of Asian Americans as punchlines or objects of ridicule reinforced their status as perpetual "foreigners" unfit for full social inclusion.

This history sets the stage for understanding civility in the realm of news media, where the evolution of news and its intersections with technology have continually reshaped public perceptions and discourse.

Historical Context of News Media

News media has never been particularly civil. From the beginning, it has been tied to political tension and advocacy. Many major newspapers in the 19th century were openly partisan, promoting the agendas and policy goals of the ruling political parties, families, and classes.

This political utility continued through various technological changes. The printing press democratized access to news, but primarily for the literate elite. Early newspapers were more about political advocacy than objective reporting. For example, the *New York Herald*, founded in 1835, heavily supported Andrew Jackson's presidency, praising his policies, such as abolishing the Bank of the United States, and reflecting anti-immigrant sentiments aligned with Jackson's base.[2]

With the emergence of broadcast and digital media in the 20th century, the landscape of news changed again. Radio and television made information and news more widely accessible to the general public, and digital media further revolutionized news by making it more instant and personalized. Both platforms wield immense power in shaping public opinion and discourse on important civic and social issues. While broadcast and digital media have democratized access to news, they have also accelerated and reinforced biases and discrimination against various marginalized communities. As expressed in a 2023 Pew survey, Black Americans see several problems in news coverage of Black people. Most respondents say that Black people are covered more negatively than people in other racial and ethnic groups.[3]

The evolution of media civility and representation of Black Americans reflect broader societal changes rather than a direct causal relationship. During the segregation era, the appearance of civility in media and politics was maintained by excluding or minimizing voices of marginalized groups, including Black

Americans. The "civility" of that time was often a facade that masked deep societal inequalities and tensions. As media and politics became more democratized and accessible, they began to reflect a wider range of societal tensions and perspectives that were previously suppressed, hidden, or ignored in mainstream discourse. Thus, the perceived decrease in media civility is the result of increased visibility of societal conflicts and tensions that were always present but previously not acknowledged in mainstream media.

Evolving Business Model of News

The so-called objectivity standard in news is a relatively modern development, emerging primarily in the 1920s and driven by business needs. As news organizations sought to differentiate themselves, they began to market themselves as purveyors of truth and facts. Ben Bagdikian, journalist, media critic, and author of *The Media Monopoly*, explains that "newspapers neutralized information for fear that strong news and views pleasing to one part of the audience might offend another part and thus reduce the circulation on which advertising rates depend."[4] This shift ushered in an era where neutrality and objectivity became fundamental principles of journalism, replacing the previously common practice of proudly partisan reporting. However, the meaning and application of objectivity in journalism continued to evolve in subsequent decades, particularly in response to challenges posed by figures like Senator Joseph McCarthy in the 1950s and more recently by President Donald Trump.[5]

In the 1980s, the introduction of cable news and the 24-hour news cycle marked another significant shift. Networks like CNN changed consumption patterns by making news a constant presence in daily life, necessitating the need to fill airtime far beyond an anchor's presentation of top stories. To sustain 24-hour coverage, cable television began incorporating more sensationalist content, featuring increasingly louder voices and more "uncivil" debates to draw viewers. Events like the 1994 O. J. Simpson car chase highlighted how news had become a form of continuous entertainment.[6] This shift necessitated a business model that prioritized engagement over objectivity, leading to the prevalence of talking heads and contentious, opinion-based content over traditional reporting, especially in cable news.

Contention has now become content. The previous model, with figures like Walter Cronkite serving as an authoritative source, no longer dominates. Instead, there is a focus shifted to "experts," whose arguments and disputes are becoming the main attraction. Inevitably, civility—defined as civilized behavior—declined, as partisan talking points and controversy became key drivers in capturing audience attention.

Digital Disruption and the Rise of Social Media

The digital revolution further transformed news media. The internet enabled 24–7 access to news, turning it into a commodity available across multiple devices. This mass industrialization of news meant that content had to compete for attention in an oversaturated market. As a result, news increasingly adopted a binary framing of good versus evil, right versus wrong, with a focus on conflict and an antagonistic framing of issues to capture and retain audience interest.

Research supports this shift, with a RAND Corporation study finding a gradual move toward more opinion-based journalism across platforms over nearly three decades.[7] Additionally, a study published in *Nature Human Behaviour* revealed that negative words in headlines increased click-through rates, demonstrating the effectiveness of contentious content in capturing audience attention in the digital age.[8]

Social media amplified these dynamics, allowing biases and sensationalism to spread faster and further. While social media is often blamed for the erosion of civility, it is merely an accelerator of preexisting trends in news media. The echo chambers created by social media platforms reflect the divisions already present in society, exacerbated by news organizations' pursuit of "clickable" content. The partisan nature of cable news, established long before social media's rise by networks like Fox News and MSNBC taking clear ideological stances, became increasingly polarized over time.[9] With the advent of social media, this preexisting partisan divide was amplified and accelerated, transforming into an even more potent and pervasive force in shaping public discourse and opinion.[10]

The Role of AI and Public Discourse

AI systems, developed by humans, inherently carry our flaws and biases. Biased data leads to biased outcomes. For example, in 2016, Microsoft's Tay.AI Twitter chatbot was manipulated into making offensive statements, highlighting the dangers of flawed or biased AI. Similarly, in 2023, Buzzfeed's "Barbies of the World" project used MidJourney, an AI imaging tool, to generate pictures of Barbie dolls from 193 countries. The results included a South Sudan Barbie with a gun and a Thailand Barbie with blonde hair, instead of the dark hair most Asians naturally have, showcasing the persistent issue of bias in artificial intelligence.[11]

However, AI also has the potential to help journalism be less biased and connect better with their audiences. For example, journalists often assume that the meaning of certain terms is universal, but different communities interpret words differently. Terms like "gun violence" or "gun mitigation" can carry different political connotations depending on one's perspective. It's crucial for journalists to recognize and contextualize these differences to provide clearer, more inclusive reporting. This approach is equally important for other contentious issues like abortion, where word choice can significantly impact public discourse.

The University of Florida is working on Authentically, a language analysis tool that leverages AI technology to help journalists understand and improve their word choices in real time.[12] Authentically's purpose is to flag potentially biased language and help newsrooms better reflect the communities they serve. The tool could help news organizations to reduce potential inflammatory or divisive languages in their coverage and contribute to a more civil public discourse.

Organizations such as the Partnership on AI, Hacks/Hackers, and the Online News Association are actively raising awareness and providing training on both the potential and pitfalls of AI.

The Business of Journalism in the Internet Age

The business model of journalism has always been tied to its ability to attract and retain audiences. Traditionally, newspapers dominated both content creation and distribution. The internet disrupted this model, decoupling content from distribution and, with its global reach, favoring scale over substance. A decreased number of major news organizations thrive in this environment, but smaller, community-focused outlets struggle and often close.

The lack of diversity among news organizations also worsens the business problem, as the next generation of news consumers finds news less relevant to their lives.[13] Despite efforts to address the diversity issue, the industry continues to fall short. This persistent lack of representation contributes to a decline in civility, as underrepresented communities feel marginalized and misunderstood, leading to frustration, distrust, and more combative discourse in the public sphere.

In 1978, the American Society of News Editors, primarily composed of newspaper companies, pledged that the percentage of minorities in newsrooms would match that of the population by 2000. However, by 2019, people of color made up only 21.9 percent of staff at newspapers and digital news sites and 25.9 percent of television news staff, while the US population of people of color had reached 38.7 percent. Additionally, more than half of those under 16 identified as a racial or ethnic minority.[14]

The question for journalism today is whether it can sustain diverse business models that prioritize serving a diverse audience with different values, such as local engagement and investigative reporting, over sheer audience numbers.

A Call to Action

The paradoxical use of "civility" as both a tool for exclusion and a demand for assimilation is rooted in who has the power and whose story gets told. Increasing diversity in media representation, challenging stereotypes, and reducing misunderstanding are some of the crucial steps towards greater societal understanding and more civil discourse. This positive future of journalism depends on the support of its audience. Quality news requires investment, whether through subscriptions, donations, or other forms of support. If we value accurate, equitable journalism, we must be willing to pay for it. Just as we subscribe to entertainment services like Netflix and Hulu, we should also support the news sources that keep us informed and engaged in our communities.

In conclusion, the interplay between technology, news media, and civility is a dynamic and ongoing process. By understanding this evolution, we can better navigate the challenges and opportunities it presents, ensuring that news media serves the public good in an increasingly digital world.

NOTES

1 Smithsonian American Art Museum, "Manifest Destiny and Indian Removal," americanexperience.si.edu.

2 National Archives, "American Elections and Campaigns—1800 to 1865: Politics in the Antebellum Press," The Reagan Library Education Blog, November 3, 2022, reagan.blogs.archives.gov.

3 Pew Research Center, "Black Americans' Experiences with News," September 26, 2023, www.pewresearch.org.

4 Sydney Forde, "The Political Economy of Journalistic Objectivity," LPE Project, September 27, 2022, lpeproject.org.

5 Matthew Pressman, "Journalistic Objectivity Evolved the Way It Did for a Reason," *Time*, November 5, 2018, time.com.

6 Brian Stelter, "How the O. J. Simpson Car Chase and Trial Changed Media Forever," *Rolling Stone*, April 12, 2024, www.rollingstone.com.

7 Jonathan S. Blake, Shawn Smith, Steven Davenport, and Mahlet G. Tebeka, "News in a Digital Age: Comparing the Presentation of News Information Across Media Platforms over Time," RAND Corporation, May 14, 2019, www.rand.org.

8 Claire E. Robertson, Nicolas Pröllochs, Karou Schwarzenegger, Philip Pärnamets, Jay J. Van Bavel, and Stefan Feuerriegel, "Negativity Drives Online News Consumption," *Nature Human Behavior* 7 (2023), https://doi.org/10.1038/s41562-023-01538-4.

9 Hailey Reissman, "Cable News Networks Have Grown More Polarized, Study Finds," Annenberg School of Communication, University of Pennsylvania, August 1, 2022, www.asc.upenn.edu.

10 Mark Jurkowitz, Amy Mitchell, Elisa Shearer, and Mason Walker, "U.S. Media Polarization and the 2020 Election: A Nation Divided," Pew Research Center, January 24, 2020, www.pewresearch.org.

11 Reena Koh, "A List of AI-Generated Barbies From 'Every Country' Gets Blasted on Twitter for Blatant Racism and Endless Cultural Inaccuracies," *Business Insider*, July 11, 2023, www.businessinsider.com.

12 Authentically, University of Florida, trust.jou.ufl.edu.

13 Lucas Galan, Jordan Osserman, Tim Parker, and Matt Taylor, "How Young People Consume News and the Implications for Mainstream Media," Reuters Institute for the Study of Journalism, University of Oxford, reutersinstitute.politics.ox.ac.uk.

14 Paul Cheung, "Journalism Should Take a Cue from Entertainment—Diversity Grows Audiences," Poynter, March 28, 2022, www.poynter.org.

From Civil Discourse to Civil Discord

How Social Media Incentivizes the Politics of Anger

IMRAN AHMED

I first came to see how social media has changed the way we conduct discourse nearly a decade ago. I was working in the British Parliament as a special adviser to the Labour Party for the Remain Campaign in the 2016 referendum on Britain's European Union membership. In that campaign, we saw disinformation about the election process, along with hate narratives against Muslims, Blacks, and Jews. Online discourse became fever pitched—and we just did not understand where these ideas and conspiracies, these narratives of hatred, were coming from.

It was toward the end of that campaign that my colleague, Jo Cox, a brilliant woman and a fantastically caring mother of two, was shot, stabbed, and beaten to death on the streets of her constituency in Batley and Spen, in Northern England.

The man who killed her, Thomas Mair, shouted as he attacked, "Britain First, death to traitors." Two years earlier, Britain First was the name of the first political movement to achieve one million likes on Facebook. When I was told by a colleague that there was something on Facebook with one million likes, some kind of crazy anti-Black, anti-Muslim organization, I remember saying to him, "Who cares? They've got a million clicks. We've got half a million members." I dismissed them.

I was wrong. Profoundly wrong. We had missed the reality that social media was becoming the primary locus of the negotiation of our social mores, the norms of attitude and behavior, and our values as a society that sustain our democracy. Even the negotiation of the corpus of information that we call facts had shifted to digital spaces, to Facebook groups, to X (formerly Twitter), to Reddit—spaces that in conventional forums like politics we didn't grasp. Not for a moment did we accept that these settings could possibly be where facts are decided, because they're decided in constituency meetings, aren't they? Or on the pages of *The Times* or *The Guardian*.

As it turns out, that assumption was nonsense.

There are three billion people on Facebook, with two billion daily users. Even with X and Instagram and TikTok—which everyone talks about because they are used by a lot of young people—Facebook remains the 800-pound gorilla in our information ecosystem. The algorithms that determine what succeeds on Facebook have more influence on humanity's understanding of each other, and of ourselves, than any news provider in human history.

Digital communications are to conventional communications platforms as the nuclear bomb is to the M16 rifle. They are operating on an entirely different scale and economics. The economic revolution that the printing press inaugurated also broadened the category of those who could control the means of production of communications. Social media, however, is like the nuclear age. It represents the production of almost unlimited amounts of communication, with zero marginal cost for every additional message sent to every additional person. When a message can be sent to and received by billions of people for the same cost as one person, the nature of communications fundamentally changes.

The calculus for the producer and distributor of information then becomes: How do I game the algorithm? It turns into a role-playing game of trying to figure out how to make the system work for you, rather than being about the quality of your arguments, or the facts within your post. It's about whether or not you've managed to make the algorithm amplify your content to as many people as possible, so you can get the eyeballs on it.

The second facet of the economic argument is that because this system is funded almost entirely by advertising, it really is just about the eyeballs: How many eyeballs can I get on my content? And how much can I sell them for? Here, engagement is the key. What makes content succeed, and what doesn't, is how engaging it is. The system is asymmetric. It's weighted toward that which induces the most emotional reaction and therefore engagement. Inevitably, it privileges content that provokes negative reactions over positive ones. This consequence is one of the biggest challenges we face in social media.

For example, if I post on X that I really love puppies—and I do—I might get a few likes. But if I post something about how much I hate puppies, thousands of people would add comments calling me a sicko and asking what's wrong with me. Users would repost me, adding "Oh, my God!, that guy really hates puppies! I told you he was horrible!!!" People start piling on. And that's engagement. My original message will be pushed to a lot more timelines because the system recognizes that my post is inducing reaction, and the algorithm starts to amplify it.

The puppy example is glib, but we have a macro example of the same phenomenon thanks to a whistleblower from Facebook, Frances Haugen. When Facebook was studying its impact on politics, the company asked political parties across Europe which of their messages were and weren't working on its platform. Facebook wanted to understand how it was changing the nature of democratic politics.

The results were terrifying. The study showed that *negative* political posts were almost the only kinds of political messaging that were working. Online content was pushing negative partisanship—how much you hate the other side—rather than positive partisanship, which is how much you love your own side. Political parties had begun to adapt and changed their messaging. Such is the devastating impact of how algorithms and business incentives have changed the way we share information and interact with each other now.

This transformation brings me to incivility and how we should approach it. Civility is a challenging concept because people like me have had to be "uncivil" by the standards of those who were dominant in society. We stand on the shoulders of those who were genuinely uncivil—who demanded their rights, especially their right to protest and to be uncivil as defined by the dominant norms—so that we can have a voice today.

What I am looking at is the structural, systemic incivility built into the means by which we communicate, and especially how our digital interactions are changing the nature of even what we believe to be true. The messages that succeed, and that we therefore see most often in our social media feeds, are the ones that are most angry. This reality triggers our frequency bias: our psychology dictates that when we see something more frequently, we think it's more "normal" and acceptable—and we begin to believe it.

This development is how we have come to see the radical and rapid resocialization of our societies to being much more angry. It's not only about Donald Trump. I've seen it in the politics of my country, the United Kingdom, on both left and right. What links Narendra Modi to Rodrigo Duterte to Jair Bolsonaro to Viktor Orbán to Jeremy Corbyn to Boris Johnson are the means by which they express their messages of anger and division.

The generated anger is fundamentally corrosive to journalism as well. If you are trying to promote your news story online, the headline and how angry the headline is matter more than the facts within, which necessarily changes the way journalists think if they want to be successful. The jobs journalists do, and the standards to which they hold themselves, are vital and potent for our society, but these new incentives gravely undermine the quality and effectiveness of the work.

There are other aspects of social media platforms that make them so dangerous. On them, disinformation holds the advantage. It is not merely not the truth. It also showcases non-falsifiable statements that cannot be disproved. You cannot, for example, disprove that Bill Gates is a lizard, and that there is a conspiracy to cover up that he is one. You cannot disprove that doctors have been systematically lying to us about the COVID vaccines, and that they are doing so because they are getting paid off by Pfizer and Merck. Because how do you actively disprove these conspiracy theories to the satisfaction of someone who believes them? It is nearly impossible.

Disinformation is the ultimate example of incivility. It represents a lack of respect for the very concept of discourse and debate. The winner of a debate should never be one of the participants; it should always be the audience. Debate and discourse should be edifying to the whole community, but we are losing that invaluable outcome because of the way these platforms force us to communicate. Function follows form. On social media, we see people arguing and shouting, with no capacity within the system for much more collaborative, discursive, deliberative spaces.

I would also like to make a point about abuse, which is powerfully reshaping our society and what we're willing to say. Online abuse—which can lead to offline intimidation and even violence—changes the rules of the game for journalists and other professionals, whose work depends on promoting factual information to the public. Take, for example, public health officials and scientists during the pandemic. I spent a lot of time working with vaccinologists and healthcare leaders who wanted to disseminate to the public the scientific facts about the coronavirus. But they knew that when they attempted to do so, they would be subject to a ton of abuse. And so some became reluctant.

Abuse has become a tool to reshape what people feel they can say. It is purposeful communication designed to silence others. Freedom of speech for abusers means restricting the freedom of speech for their victims, which is why it is really important that we have rules for social media platforms, just as we do in other aspects of discourse in our world—and that those rules are enforced. Social media platforms require users to agree to community standards, but the companies do not enforce them. And why should they? It's cheaper for them to do nothing, allow the car crash to occur, and then monetize the attention devoted to the crash. To have enforced rules of discourse would require social media companies to develop a genuine code of ethics for control of these platforms. But, of course, the industry's incentives are lined up to do the opposite. The current business model is all about the engagement. It's all about the eyeballs. It's all about the advertising. And, in the end, it's all about the dollars.

Nothing makes a stronger case for the necessity of diversity within the technology sector. In order to have more ethics in social media and AI, we need a broader base of people thinking about these issues. There's no tech solution to the tech problems we have, because at their core they're not really technology problems. They're ethical problems, they're moral problems, they're questions of what we choose to profit from, of what we choose to accept.

Hate is a virus that looks for a vulnerable host. Right now, it has found a body where it can breed. It is taking advantage of the fact that social media lacks an adequate immune system, but offers instead essentially ungoverned spaces and imposes no consequences. Hate actors can promulgate their views with impunity and spread them exponentially, infecting the rest of society as well. Structural, systemic incivility and lack of respect, which social media platforms encourage us to adopt, threaten everything we've built. The destruction of our information ecosystem is leading to a crisis of epistemic anxiety, which leads to more conspiracy thinking, which leads to the breakdown in trust, which leads to the breakdown in our capacity to sustain our democracies.

If we fail to check it, the edifices we constructed in society to protect the dissemination of information, encouragement of discourse, and promotion of cooperation will be shattered. And that is how a civilization, even one as powerful and seemingly entrenched as ours, can be irrecoverably and even fatally damaged.

PART V

Lessons from Arts and Culture

Civility or Control?

Who Is Part of the Community?

HUSSEIN RASHID

Often, when I'm asked to respond to a concept, I start by trying to understand the etymology of the word. Trained in area studies and basic philology, I begin by exploring how *parole* is used in *langue*. To enter into a civil conversation is to be clear on the parameters within which everyone is operating.

My starting text is Raymond Williams's *Keywords*. He has no entry for "civil," "civility," or even "citizen." These terms are all subsumed under the term "civilization." For many years, both "civility" and "civilization" had overlapping meanings and would often be used interchangeably. Both referred to the domain of interactions among citizens, rather than between citizens and the state. The initial distinction was in the realm of law, between what was considered civil (citizen) and what was considered criminal (state). "Civility" became an expression of an ordered *community*. Eventually, both "civilization" and "civility" stopped referring to processes and began to refer to states of being, often in contradistinction to "barbarity" and "savagery," respectively.[1]

Thus, I enter this conversation to consider the implications of treating "civility" as a state of being that has impacts on the citizens in a community, specifically in the context of the United States. This approach also allows me to consider "incivility" as something that can exist only in contrast to a state of civility. I would argue that the existence of incivility proves that civility as a state of being is not sustainable.

If civility is the state of an ordered community, we must question who does the ordering, who is ordered, and who benefits from the particular way a community is ordered. In religious studies, scholars like Tomoko Masuzawa and David Chidester have demonstrated how "civilization" became a justification for colonialism and empire, and how the idea of religion was ordered by colonizers to support this justification.[2] Of course, race was also ordered by these same colonizers to support it, demonstrating that to turn "civilization" into a state of being is to make a marker and expression of power.[3] I contend that civility, as a state, is the enforcement of social power structures and hierarchies. That enforcement is carried out by those in power, who treat violations of civility as a rationale for the discipline of the powerless.

Since civility is to be in the service of citizens of a community, it follows that only those who can set the bounds of civility and benefit from civility are true citizens. Individuals who cannot contribute to the norms of civility, but are still bound by them, are not full citizens. They may be conditional citizens, contingent citizens, or second-class citizens. Incivility is a rupture of the norm, an exposure of the discipline, and a claim at citizenship. It is the momentary dissolution of barriers, a passing carnivalization, that exposes the discipliner and the disciplined, exchanging their roles for the briefest of periods. That upending of the expected order is a threat to the discipliner and an opportunity for the disciplined.

Among the most well-known of recent public acts of "incivility" in the United States is Colin Kaepernick's act of civil disobedience. A professional football player for the San Francisco 49ers, he took a knee during the performance of the US national anthem in

2016. Since 2001, there has been an increase in performative patriotism and displays of militarism at professional football games. The performance includes the expectation that the players will stand with their hands over their hearts during the national anthem. His actions were a protest to bring attention to police brutality and violence against Black communities and other communities of color. As though anticipating the critique he would get—that he hates America—he framed his initial response very carefully, saying: "I have great respect for the men and women that have fought for this country. . . . I have family, I have friends that have gone and fought for this country. And they fight for freedom, they fight for the people, they fight for liberty and justice, for everyone. That's not happening. People are dying in vain because this country isn't holding their end of the bargain up, as far as giving freedom and justice, liberty to everybody."[4]

Kaepernick is very specific in his critique. While he could make a connection between unchecked police powers, the militarization of the police departments, and the military-industrial complex, he chooses instead to align himself with the US military to expose hypocrisy in policing. He casts the mission of the US military in terms of (aspirational) ideals, and notes that those ideals are not being realized by policing. He also makes clear in other venues that the form of his protest—kneeling—was crafted in consultation with US military veterans who did not consider the act disrespectful to them or to the flag.

Kaepernick's move places him in a larger American racial discourse, demanding an alignment between the ideals and realities of the US. For example, Langston Hughes's poem "Let America be America Again" addresses the promise of the United States and the nature of discrimination in the country as being violently at odds. Yet Hughes does not abandon that promise. Instead, he sees it as a challenge. The penultimate verse of the poem reads:

> O, yes,
> I say it plain,
> America never was America to me,
> And yet I swear this oath—
> America will be![5]

Despite Kaepernick's care, the preparation he did, and his continuation of a tradition of protest against the *actions* of the United States for the sake of the *ideals* of the United States, his narrative was still framed by his critics as disrespectful and borderline treasonous. These critics, many of whom were on social media, feeding into mainstream reactionary political discourse, sought to frame Kaepernick's actions as outside the norms of civil and acceptable behavior. This framing continues to enforce racial norms and second-class citizenship for minoritized groups in the US.[6] In recent years, civility became the force to shut down critique of racial hierarchy, even as protests for Black Lives Matter were becoming more widespread. Protests in sports for racial equity are not new. In the 1968 Mexico Summer Olympics, Tommie Smith won the gold medal and John Carlos won the bronze medal in the 200-meter dash. As the US national anthem played during the medal ceremony, they each raised one hand as a fist in support of the movement for Black equality in the US. They were criticized heavily in the media at the time for upending the norms of national sporting competition. In 1967, Muhammad Ali, a famous boxer, refused to serve as a soldier in the US war against Vietnam, again citing the poor treatment of Blacks in the US. His rupture of civility resulted in a felony conviction for refusing to be drafted. While both these older acts, and numerous others, were subject to contemporaneous approbation, they are more recently held up as important examples of civil disobedience, even as Kaepernick is condemned for a similar style of protest.

In the fictional worlds of the Marvel Cinematic Universe, the movie *Captain Marvel* highlights demands placed on women to please men. Brie Larson plays the eponymous hero, whose civilian name is Carol Danvers. At one point, a man tells her to smile. She refuses and is harangued by the man for not acquiescing to his whims. She takes his hand, suggesting a reconciliation, before using her super strength to crush it. Then, she offers an exchange: if he gives her his motorcycle, helmet, and jacket, he can keep his hand. As he does so, she asks him for a smile.

The scene is clearly an acknowledgment of the ask of women to always smile for men. There is also a suggestion that the scene was included by the film's directors in response to men who were critiquing the movie before its release because Larson was not smiling in the trailer.[7] The character of Danvers is enacting incivility by not agreeing to a demand placed on her, one specifically related to an expectation of public behavior, and then, in another act of incivility, by exercising her power over her accoster, power he was not expecting her to have. Her final act of incivility is asking him for a smile.

This scene is crafted as an absolute inversion of power. The act of incivility here is not de novo, a new attempt to generate conversations about power that have lapsed. Rather, it is in the carnivalesque—not only the collapse of the boundaries between the supposedly powerful and the supposedly powerless, but the granting of power to the person perceived as powerless. Like the classic work of science fiction *Sultana's Dream,* it is the preposterousness of the powerless doing what the powerful do that exposes the discipline imposed on female-presenting bodies.[8]

In both these examples, Kaepernick and *Captain Marvel,* acts of incivility serve as challenges to the social order that disciplines and controls minoritized bodies. Kaepernick's actions are also explicitly an ethical spectacle. According to Stephen Duncombe, a progressive ethical spectacle is "one that is directly democratic, breaks down hierarchies, fosters community, allows for diversity, and engages with reality while asking what new realities might be possible."[9] Such spectacles are reproducible, much like Kaepernick's actions, which is why I am hesitant to consider the scene from *Captain Marvel* an example.

The issue of the ethical spectacle is instrumental in understanding how incivility can serve to challenge norms and structures of exclusion. Here, it is worth considering if the neo-Nazi marches that have become increasingly common in the United States since at least 2015 are acts of incivility. These marches are almost never described in the same way as Kaepernick's actions. They are not reported on as disrespectful or treasonous. While they may be described as disruptive or illegal and even abhorrent, they are nonetheless generally reported on as acceptable. The history of marches in support of white supremacy are historically normative and do not threaten the implicit social order in the same way that Kaepernick's explicit challenges do. Arguably, their presence and actions highlight the idea that civility is simply a vehicle to maintain the status quo of power. However, if we were to read these marches as incivility, then we have to ask if they, too, are seeking a change in social norms and structures.

The use of the term ethical spectacle to describe Kaepernick's actions gives us a way to think constructively of the Nazi marches in the context of civility. Duncombe posits the idea of the fascist spectacle, which is "overtly political and inherently collective. The ideal conjured up is one of mass obedience and a sacrifice of the individual to a higher will."[10] The expression of fascist ideals, constructed around a collective White identity, would strike no one as unusual in the history of the US, nor would the affinity between the US racial system and Nazi ideals.[11] These marches are not for a new vision of belonging, but are the desire to maintain the order as it stands. They are about an absolute belief in a stratified American society and a reaction to ethical spectacles that demand a United States of possibilities of inclusion. The marchers are marchers of civility; their calls are to not change anything. While the United States may not be an explicitly racist country, structural racism permeates it. The neo-Nazi marches may be too extreme in their explicitness, but they are simply manifestations of how the social and political system was designed.

This understanding of civility is inherently pessimistic, and I think rightfully so. Without the recognition of how civility is weaponized, it cannot be recovered to serve as a space to bring citizens together. As Americans, we need to understand how we can participate in debate, dialogue, and disagreement in ways that result in productive and generative resolution. Civility, as it stands now, hastens polarization and division. Parties cannot engage with one another as long as the implicit starting point by one of the parties is the preservation of current power systems.

Perhaps, then, the civil thing to do is ask, "Who benefits?" This question can be applied to the current system, a change in the system, and the impacts of a system. Currently, civility is a system of power analysis, and that system should be clear and transparent. Instead, civility needs to return to being a process, one that is dynamic and allows us to cultivate a more inclusive and equitable community. Then, perhaps, it can be the fascists we will cast out of the social order for being uncivil, not those we say are part of the social order but whom we treat as outcasts.

> O, yes,
> I say it plain,
> America never was America to me,
> And yet I swear this oath—
> America will be![12]

NOTES

1 Raymond Williams, *Keywords: A Vocabulary of Culture and Society* (Oxford University Press, 1985), 57–60.

2 David Chidester, *Empire of Religion: Imperialism and Comparative Religion* (University of Chicago Press, 2014); Tomoko Masuzawa, *The Invention of World Religions: Or, How European Universalism Was Preserved in the Language of Pluralism* (University of Chicago Press, 2005).

3 Nikole Hannah-Jones, *The 1619 Project: A New Origin Story* (One World, 2021); Ibram X. Kendi, *Stamped from the Beginning: The Definitive History of Racist Ideas in America* (Nation, 2016).

4 Quoted in Steph Doehler, "Taking the Star-Spangled Knee: The Media Framing of Colin Kaepernick," *Sport in Society* 26, no. 1 (2023): 46.

5 Langston Hughes, *The Collected Poems of Langston Hughes*, ed. Arnold Rampersad and David E. Roessel (Vintage, 1995), 191.

6 For further discussion of media framing and race, see Shane M. Graber, Ever J. Figueroa, and Krishnan Vasudevan, "Oh, Say, Can You Kneel: A Critical Discourse Analysis of Newspaper Coverage of Colin Kaepernick's Racial Protest," *Howard Journal of Communications* 31, no. 5 (2020): 464–80.

7 María José Gámez Fuentes, "Breaking the Logic of Neoliberal Victimhood: Vulnerability, Interdependence and Memory in Captain Marvel (Anna Boden and Ryan Fleck, 2019)," *European Journal of Cultural Studies* 24, no. 1 (2021): 101, 105.

8 Rokeya Sakhawat Hossain, *Sultana's Dream and Selections from The Secluded Ones* (Feminist Press, 1988).

9 Stephen Duncombe, *Dream: Re-Imagining Progressive Politics in an Age of Fantasy* (New Press, 2007), 126.

10 Duncombe, *Dream*, 124.

11 James Q. Whitman, *Hitler's American Model: The United States and the Making of Nazi Race Law* (Princeton University Press, 2018).

12 Hughes, *Collected Poems*, 191.

Civility

A Prose Poem

RICARDO ALBERTO MALDONADO

What I propose to share and land upon, for the time being, came to me with a thundering force at a literature conference by the end of summer 2023. It was not granting text—the purpose of our congress in September—but rather, a chance to demonstrate an essence of myself. I mean: granting seems the object of aspiration for much of my activity, as I put stock in the potential of generosity.

I am Ricardo Alberto Maldonado: a poet, of course, a translator from Puerto Rico, and a president of an academy—these substantives grant me allegiances to architecture, both physical and digital, and a certain proclivity for giving to the field of literature and its community. I have accrued value by way of allegiances, accrued enough so as to be able to make a living of my intersections in the art of letters and meditate through them a project, a life assignment.

It concerns me, where I attempt to comprehend and decode the function of civility and the question of literature as they come to my life: that my humanity came to me with words, even when I was young, and I found in reading a conspiracy, that is: a way for living. I attempt to make myself a case study—or study of a special case—on how civility could play out and why. I don't propose to answer the challenges of the now, because I have made home a constant and a kind of possibility that is attuned to a collective listening of our past, our present, and the future. I want to give you something along the lines of "I bring myself to you," which one gives on the occasion of a chance meeting, sensing familiarity like a swan made of felt, like Neruda would have it, to give you an image of a thing that you can consume, take with you. I am, of course, in the thingness of metaphor.

Let me translate the atmosphere of my beginning. I was raised in Guaynabo, Puerto Rico—that is, a name that it is popularly said to mean in Taíno: "Here is another place of fresh water." And by the freshwater, in a literal sense, I grew up with three siblings, two parents (one a lawyer who never practiced; the other a sales manager for GE who was beloved, till he died and after, he was loved. I was 18).

Home was a house made of cement with windows and doors and outside, my mother's trees. Home was the locks that made it home. Home was felt. It had a loving geometry, and because it proposed a perimeter, it had a citizenship and praxis, which we translate into belonging. And home kept up during María and that's how my family "survived" a tempest: without power for three months, a relatively short sentence by the standards of recovery—short but endured, nonetheless.

I was in New York when my family had something sturdy to hold against the weather, and outside there was a wind. Then the radio stations gave out to the locomotive in the air and power went out. It was 5 a.m.; rainwater filtering in—enough to make them fear. And afterward, a neighbor looped a cord to my mother's fridge to keep things fresh to consume. But they had a kind of power not many had, before light would come to the archipelago of Puerto Rico. Here light did not translate into power, because my people hungered in their eyes. And in their belly, they hungered. But America sent cameras, because there was a document of horror to translate and file into an archive. We meditate so vividly on national television.

Once asked to take remedial English; twice in Brooklyn, I was labeled *Spic*: that charge in the tongue I did poems with, as I wrote in English since I chanced upon Housmann's "To an Athlete Dying Young," gave shape to the performance of civility: in corduroy and slacks, and my Converse shoes I was, I believe, subject to an American dissertation of which I was, among many things, a reader of an atmosphere.

I was a Ricardo. I sat, I observed, I felt a blunt end of how I was subject to perception and how I performed it. And it conquered me: Spic, they called me on the F train in 2005. Spic also in Park Slope; that was later. It was not imprecise to suggest I had lost value and felt, therefore, untranslated into the language of a city. I administered my living and measured myself that pound of sorrow. That night, for me, the Great American Century Perished, but I kept to my living between stations, under the surface. For I work in literature and I had made it, of course, in New York.

The power of literature lives through our collective inquiry. I was a teacher, in my time, nearly twenty years ago, that to be a writer I felt one had to teach; and to teach one must understand the poem to give shape to what was previous and unsayable. Added to a curriculum: the moment of composition, I supposed, was a mercy to be made with the possibility of words. And so I instructed that the project of literature felt such: to know with faith that we are not alone; that we have made ourselves legible to project ourselves to the page; that we had to dream our own canon of literatures forward. It was my writer's temperament that sought to loosely reference Heaney's naming at the Nobel, to "seek devotion to things" and make a home: to spell corroboration with what was going on in the "suspension between the archaic and the modern," as Heaney termed his youth, that we are all participants in the human project and susceptible to it.

Power, of course, legislates, as it is wont to do: "Foreign to the United States in a domestic sense," pronounced Justice Henry Brown, about Puerto Rico, at the Supreme in 1901. This was, I swear, a judicial clarification.

What concerns me as a poet has been how the law translates subjects of collective sovereignty. In literature, we would label the activity an advancement of a plot. "The land was ours before we were the land's. / She was our land more than a hundred years / Before we were her people," wrote Robert Frost. Or put another way, he landed, at inauguration, toward the advancement of a literary empire.

Soon after the hurricane, I began to write in Spanish to make myself so foreign in my domesticity: I was a Spic, for I sensed all the subjects America had my wildness on me as I had been taught His Majesty's language, but I, too, masticated Spanish. Spanish over my tongue. With it I could read the surface of my land as coarse and difficult because home was such. And that's how I peopled my land. The people as I felt them had a home that was precarious but ours.

"Ricardo, we read your manuscript with great interest, but don't think it's quite right for us or quite ready for us. We were attracted to its intellectualism, the thinking lyric, its urbanity, but wanted to see something a bit more savage or wild," so was the project of edition that received my work; the words waited for me, in 2016, when I inquired with my manuscript, more than a decade after arrival: "More savage. Wild." I would be read thus.

By nature the mind wants to argue against, and put a word where a word has put us out. That's a funny way of saying it has been an interest of mine to spell out one fact toward poetry for the edification of civics for a life.

I want to suggest that rather than a totalizing force, a tract could be proposed for the chance of poetry as art that makes it porous enough in community to force a different kind of moral accuracy—which is a way of posting value on a particular ground for agility that incites negotiation against blank space.

One writes with, even when one writes against. As Louis Zukofsky has it, "Talk is a form of love / Let us talk." Literature is a project of interrogating that privileges how a lyric may respond to the moral demands a citizen may find of our great unknowing, especially when utility remains indisputably obscure. Truth informs our shared obligations. That may be, on my end, the only project that may ring true for me, at any rate, sustaining the prosody of the medium itself. Not the performance of civility, merely, but mutual regard, a stronger obligation.

Comedy as a Tool of Civility

Why and How Humor Humanizes and Connects

CATY BORUM

In the heyday of his 1970s entertainment empire, Norman Lear, the legendary TV creator, writer, and activist—and my mentor, as luck and the universe would have it—delighted in a frenzied production schedule that easily would have felled a less energetic soul. At one point, a handful of the most-watched sitcoms on American television were created or cocreated by Norman, and he attended nearly every live audience taping. He relished the comedy writers' room—the communal sketchpad where funny people played their way to a workable script—but it was the audience that captured his heart.

For Norman, there was nothing quite like watching a group of assembled humans—varied by age, race, ethnicity, religion, regional affiliation, and social class—as a joke landed in real time. They rocked forward and rolled back in their seats, as he described it, as a solo body lost in raucous, delighted glee.[1] Norman talked frequently about this wave of laughter that rippled in unison—a tiny victory of momentary togetherness, conjoining individual lives in shared joy and silliness, regardless of whatever emotional baggage or disagreements or grief they brought with them. And the fact that his shows dug into taboo topics, from racism to gender equity to war and homophobia? Well, that was the entire point—"the foolishness of the human condition," as he liked to say.[2] Comedy and suffering dance together.

Cut to decades later. It's late October 2023, and my collaborators and I are backstage in Los Angeles at Dynasty Typewriter, an old vaudeville theater transformed into a popular Hollywood comedy club. We're about to launch the first public show of our initiative, called the *Yes, And . . . Laughter Lab*, which lifts up, supports, and showcases diverse comedians who find their humor in the ridiculous absurdity of the human experience, sharing stories and lived realities all too often marginalized or dehumanized in mainstream American entertainment.[3] History will remind us of this moment's trauma, three weeks after a horrific terrorist attack devolved into war in the Middle East, displayed throughout the world across news and social media. And so, as the show prepares to start, we are a little nervous. Our initiative, after all, is not frivolous comedy, but humor about topics that are tender, fraught, complex. How will the audience respond?

One by one, a wildly disparate assemblage of comedians takes to the stage: among others, there's Lorena Russi, the Latinx former soccer player talking about her "gay divorce"; Becky Braunstein, who publicly reveals her cancer diagnosis on stage for the first time; Meredith Casey, killing it in a true-story routine about mental illness; Mohamed Kheir, skewering Islamophobia; Woody Fu, charming the room with the eccentricities of his father's habit of collecting, well, everything; and Dylan Adler, whose song-and-dance number is a dazzling display of total absurdity and legitimate Broadway chops.

The audience goes wild. Floods of laughter rush through the theater—those familiar tides of communal recognition and release, physical embodiments of our shared humanity, pain, and messiness.

Norman was right.

Among forms of cultural expression at our disposal, comedy is one of our most precious tools of civility. The act of "being civil," after all, is intentional—civility requires us to see and contemplate one another, regardless of our differences, and genuinely seek to understand even the most basic shared human experience. Incivility, on the other hand, is divisive. We are not the same when we are enmeshed in incivility—not equally human, not equally deserving of basic dignity or respect. Only one point of view is valued when we are not practicing civility. And at its worst, incivility tells us that only one perspective is even *possible* or true.

Civility requires a kind of radical listening—and comedy is often well-equipped for the task, as comedian James Adomian once said: "Part of the magic of comedy is that you can force people who disagree with you—or even hate you—you can force them to listen."[4] None of us are perfect at this job of hearing and seeing each other across differences, but we might learn a thing or two from comedy. To be clear, comedy can also be used as a tool to practice incivility—through mockery and punching down—and as with all cultural forms, context and motivation and intention matter.

I come to this lens and work honestly, I like to say, not only because of Norman's tutelage years ago, but from my own propensity for clowning around, well established from an early age. As a professional journey, about a decade ago, I began an agenda in research and creative production to ask and answer a few basic questions: How can we find new ways to encourage ourselves and others to learn, feel, and engage with people, lived realities, and social problems that may not be our own, or about which we disagree? When it comes to engaging people in wicked social challenges, how can we get them to listen and see some element of human connection and shared solidarity that might energize a desire to solve them together?

At face value, these are not original questions, of course, but they came with a theory about what might be missing. Instinctively (see: I was a funny kid, above), I was both curious and frustrated about the extent to which the most dedicated sectors that often help drive movements toward progressive social change and equity—civil society and philanthropy chief among them—didn't seem to take comedy seriously. Several books, creative production projects, and many hours with comedians later, I like to think I've answered some of my original questions in a summative way: through comedy, we open a portal to see our flaws and absurdity, and thus, our shared humanity. And it is in these small spaces where we can find one another.

How does this work, though? Why is comedy a tool of civility, and how can its core ingredients help us embody civility in our own practices of being human? There are meaningful lessons to be unpacked in understanding why we laugh at jokes and silliness, how comedy is made, and how humor serves audiences in functional ways.

Comedy at Work

Comedy is and always has functioned as a form of social critique and societal rebuke; often, this is where our contemplation of the topic begins and ends.[5] Reflections on comedy's greater purpose span disciplines of scholarship and track back many generations—reason alone to take the subject seriously—to folks like Aristotle and Freud, who both wrote and spoke of humor's functions for civilized society: to point out absurdity, to act as catharsis and a cultural corrective.[6] Humor is meaningful in virtually every culture, a rhetorical coping tool for oppressed peoples, a source of resilience and connection, and often one of the only ways to make it through a taboo topic. But to think about comedy as merely a mechanism to highlight societal wrongs is to miss its magic as a way to encourage civility. Because its core ingredients are play and creativity, comedy is also a source of civic imagination: it allows us to imagine a world that could exist—and to strive for such a world, even if it hasn't manifested quite yet.[7] For us to arrive there, we have to at least hear and listen when perhaps we might normally have a hard time, were comedy not the vehicle through which some new insight or way of seeing the world has been delivered.

When we think about how comedy "works," consider first why we laugh when we hear a good joke or quip. There are several theories that help us understand this process, which is both emotional and cognitive, but incongruity seems most relevant here.[8] Whether the funny bit is a formal joke or simply a silly situation, the unexpected nature of where it all goes—the twist at the end of a small story—is what lands the giggle. In other words, the setup is the status quo—describing something we might recognize together within a shared culture—but the laugh comes when a skilled humorist bends that reality in the form of a punchline or the payoff of the funny scenario. We laugh because of something unexpected. Where we land is a point that is incongruent with the reality of something as it exists—often, wildly and absurdly so. But recognizing the incongruity that comes within a joke or funny situation also requires a modicum of shared cultural understanding.[9] This explains why, for example, an audience of Americans might have a hard time understanding or laughing at the particulars of a political stand-up set in India, even as they might certainly understand the broad hilarity of political satire more generally.

Herein lie some of the civility possibilities that can come through comedy: we can feel, even momentarily, as if we are "the same" even when we might not be (or we perceive we aren't). If we laugh at the same joke, we are communicating—at a basic human level—that we are similar enough as human beings to crack up at the same idea. Corey Ryan Forrester, a comedian from Georgia with whom I've worked several times, talks about touring in the conservative Deep South. As a Southerner born and raised, he can connect easily with an audience that may sound and look like him: there are jokes about lactose intolerance and Southern "memaws" and funny insider bits. But then, after establishing common ground, he can also guide the audience gently into anti-racism jokes, territory that may otherwise feel a bit more taboo or painful. In this way, Forrester is a covert and trusted messenger, leveraging the trust generated by shared laughter to sneak in a few topics that may feel fraught when communicated by a more somber pathway.[10]

Another key ingredient in the idea of "comedy as a tool of civility" is the process by which comedians create and shape their work for audiences to enjoy. By the time we—the audience—experience comedy in the entertainment marketplace, as in a stand-up performance or TV show, the material has been through a lot. Failure and "bombing" are almost requirements to get a joke right, and a skilled comedian may perform the same joke many times for different audiences, tweaking and trying out what works based on deep listening. It's a reciprocal process, in other words. Audiences participate in shaping the joke by their responses, and comedians listen and reshape. Consider, also, the comedy writers' room that serves as the backbone to so much entertainment TV. In the writers' room, the individuals who craft the story and jokes pitch ideas to one another, punching up a bit here and there, traveling on a journey that mandates wild, open creativity and lack of judgment on the way to the final material. And the shaping comes from the minds of many divergent thinkers—optimally, from diverse backgrounds—who must together find the shared understanding that is sufficient to land somewhere coherent and hilarious. Civility is baked into the creative process of making comedy—radical listening, finding common ground, stripping away confusing complexity in order to arrive at cultural touchpoints that will get a laugh from audiences that may be equally diverse in their identities and lived experiences.

Finally, comedy serves important functions for us as people, beyond social critique and establishing connection. Often, humor may be the best way into a topic that might feel unfamiliar or divisive. We can laugh at jokes while we consider ideas we hadn't contemplated, or perhaps were unable to see, given humans' propensity to develop calcified positions on a wide range of topics with which we don't have firsthand experience. In this way, comedy can help us to practice and broaden our civic imaginations, or the world we might be able to create and cocreate together if we could simply see and imagine it first. When we can meet in a place of play, we come back to our shared experience—and thus, civility can be established, at least temporarily.

In the Peabody Award-winning HBO comedy series *Somebody Somewhere*, we meet Fred, a trans man who falls in love and marries a woman. The shared humanity of love and adoration is the centerpiece of their storyline, which is stripped of divisive political commentary about trans or gay marriage and rights. The civic imagination allows us to engage joyfully in a fictional world that treats Fred and his fiancée with dignity and love, and the comedy helps us stay in the shared human experience of finding someone to love and care for.

Civility demands that we bring our best selves to interactions, even when fraught or not familiar to us. When we are displaying "civility," we are, whether knowingly or unintentionally, trying to answer the question "How do we belong together?" and, perhaps more importantly, "How *can* we?" At its very essence, through play and radical listening, comedy can give us the tools and power, even if briefly, to find one another across divides, imagined or real.

NOTES

1 I wrote about this more extensively in Caty Borum, *The Revolution Will Be Hilarious: Comedy for Social Change and Civic Power* (New York University Press, 2023), 194–95.

2 Norman Lear, foreword to Caty Borum Chattoo and Lauren Feldman, *A Comedian and an Activist Walk into a Bar: The Serious Role of Comedy in Social Justice* (University of California Press, 2020), xi.

3 See Yes, and . . . Laughter Lab, www.yesandlaughterlab.com.

4 *Stand Up Planet* (2014), www.pbssocal.org.

5 See Jeffrey P. Jones, *Entertaining Politics: Satiric Television and Political Engagement* (Rowman & Littlefield, 2010); see also Borum Chattoo and Feldman, *Comedian and an Activist.*

6 For more details on comedy's societal functions, as explicated by Aristotle and Freud and others, see Borum Chattoo and Feldman, 25–29.

7 I write extensively about comedy as civic imagination, and core ingredients of play and open creativity, in Borum, *Revolution Will Be Hilarious,* 106–10.

8 Rod A. Martin, *The Psychology of Humor: An Integrative Approach* (Academic Press, 2007); Thomas R. Schultz, "A Cognitive-Development Analysis of Humor," in *Humor and Laughter: Theory, Research, and Applications,* ed. Anthony J. Chapman and Hugh C. Foot (Transaction, 1996), 11–36; Mary K. Rothbart, "Incongruity, Problem-Solving, and Laughter," in *Humor and Laughter,* Chapman and Foot, eds. (Transaction, 1996), 37; Simon Critchley, *On Humour* (Routledge, 2011), 4.

9 See Borum, *Revolution Will Be Hilarious,* 40–41.

10 Borum, 100–101.

Afterword

LYNNE P. BROWN
Chair of the NYU Brademas Center

"You'd better keep a civil tongue in your head, young lady," was my grandmother's caution whenever I uttered a snide or disrespectful comment. And while I was not sure exactly what a "civil tongue" entailed, I got the point. In fact, I grew up, personally and professionally, aspiring to an ideal of civility in my language and in my dealings with others. In all that time, however, I never really *examined* the concept: What exactly did it mean to speak or act or think in a civil manner? Is civility mainly a matter of individual behavior? Or is it also a social and political construct? If it conflicts with other worthy aims, such as freedom of expression or advancing social justice, what is its appropriate role? How best to balance competing goods?

Seeking answers to these questions (as well as others) is what motivated the John Brademas Center of New York University to undertake what we called "The Civility Project": a series of public panels, five in all, engaging a broad array of scholars, political actors, journalists, artists, and advocates. This book collects their insights and offers a rich and varied menu to sample and savor.

Taken as a whole, the project surfaced several interesting insights. For one thing, it turns out that the concept and practice of civility is far from static, either throughout American history or even in the present tense. It can be a slippery term and hard to pin down, depending on who is invoking it and to what end. Civility is best examined from several vantage points, with guides from many disciplines and in the spirit of taking a journey that might not result in a single destination.

The Brademas Center was drawn to this project because of our mission and our legacy. The Center is named after John Brademas, who was for 22 years a member of the US Congress and who then became president of New York University. In Washington, John rose to a leadership position in the House of Representatives. In that role, he could be a fierce advocate for the causes he believed in. But he was also deeply devoted to the legislative process and the prospect that seasoned and reasoned discourse could prevail across a wide political spectrum. He brought that perspective with him as president of NYU, believing there was a special place for universities in conducting informed debates among differing views.

A project of this scope could not have been undertaken without the support of many actors. First and foremost, the panelists (turned essayists) themselves, who contributed their time and talent to this enterprise. Their erudition and commitment are evident on every page.

To the JM Kaplan Fund and members of the Advisory Council of the Brademas Center, deep thanks for their generous financial contributions to the cause. Ellyn Toscano, a member of the Council, was our mainstay in helping to conceptualize the project. Collaborating with the Center's research director, Michael DiNiscia, they together developed compelling topics and identified speakers, and then planned the five events. Working with the authors and Nessa Rapoport, our talented consulting editor, Ellyn and Michael oversaw the process of turning presentations into the essays as they appear here. And all involved were models of civility throughout that process!

The Center's Tom McIntyre and Polly Terzian were the maestros of the webinars who worked to get out the word about each of the panels and oversee the technology that made sure the words were heard.

As always, it is a joy to collaborate with the professionals at the NYU Press. One of the many aims of this book is to ensure that the Press feels proud of the decision to publish it.

For all of us who had a hand in conceptualizing the initial version of the project, our aim was straightforward: to shed light on an important and relevant topic of our time. By the end, we found ourselves not only educated but questioning our own assumptions and preconceptions of what civility is and the role it plays in our personal, civic, and social lives.

We present this work to you, the readers, in the hope that you, too, may be not only enlightened but entertained and even provoked. Back to my grandmother: a civil tongue in one's head is fine, but not as valuable as a novel or stirring thought.

Acknowledgments

First and foremost, we owe our deepest gratitude to all the essayists in this volume. We challenged them to examine civility in our time, and they approached the subject with seriousness, curiosity, rigor, and enthusiasm. We thank them for their fortitude in this effort and for their generosity of ideas. And we are honored to share their deep and reasoned arguments with the readers of this volume.

We benefited from the insights of several scholars and practitioners who joined our writers in a series of online panels. Ulrich Baer, Julie Fernandes, Chenjerai Kumanyika, and Gaye Theresa Johnson helped advance the debate around the benefits and deficiencies of civility. Along with our audiences, who consistently posed pointed and thought-provoking questions, they expanded our understanding of the topic.

This book would not have been possible without the strong commitment of the John Brademas Center of New York University. We were inspired in our work by the Center's founder, John Brademas, a model of public service throughout his tenure in Congress and at NYU. And we took to heart the mission he bequeathed the Center—"bringing thinkers and doers together"—to drive deep conversations about the theory and practice of civility, culminating in these essays.

We are immensely grateful to the members of the Brademas Center Advisory Council. They offered counsel on content, suggestions for participants, and encouragement from the very start. In addition, we were very fortunate to have funding support from the JM Kaplan Fund for this initiative.

The guiding hand of the Brademas Center is Lynne Brown, former executive director and now chair of the Advisory Council. As we recoiled from the events of January 6, Lynne charged us with finding a way for the Center to make some contribution to lowering the temperature of our overheated politics. She engaged with us throughout the project, sharing her wisdom and advice, along with a proper dose of prodding to keep us moving down the path.

We had wonderful support from all our colleagues at the Brademas Center—Steve Heuer, Tom McIntyre, and Polly Terzian. But we are truly indebted to Nessa Rapoport, the Center's consulting editor. She provided counsel in the initial design of the project and then worked meticulously with us and each of our writers throughout the editorial process. She brought a wordsmith's eye for language and a granular attention for detail to editing each of the essays. The result is the clarity of prose you find on the pages here, making for a book we hope is useful to scholars and students, but also accessible to the general public. And Nessa accomplished all of this in the spirit of friendship and solidarity, which any collaborator would be privileged to have.

NYU Press is one of the finest and most supportive publishers in the academic field. We are so grateful to Ellen Chodosh and her team, who expressed interest in the project from its earliest stages, always ready with a word of encouragement about the timeliness of the topic. We much appreciate the support of Ellen, as well as of our editor, Eric Zinner, and Furqan Sayeed, our editorial assistant. Thanks to them, we are able to reach as broad an audience as possible with these ideas—students and teachers, activists, scholars, policymakers, and well informed readers.

• • •

Michael would also like to thank all the friends and family, especially his wife, Chris, who supported him with kindness, good humor, and encouragement as he wrestled civility into submission—submission of the manuscript to the publisher, that is. And a special thanks to Lucas, Remy, Marlowe, and Goodwin—his "coworkers" on those days he was editing or writing from home—for their purr-fect companionship.

• • •

Ellyn would also like to extend a personal thanks to Lynne Brown, who, over so many years has been a source of wisdom, calm and considered advice, and uncommon and fierce humor. I am forever grateful for our friendship, which I truly treasure. Thank you.

• • •

And thank you, dear reader, for making it to the end with us.

About the Editors

MICHAEL F. DINISCIA serves as Director of Research & Strategic Initiatives at the John Brademas Center of New York University, overseeing the center's research projects, international conferences, and strategic partnerships. He is coeditor, with Alberta Arthurs, of *Are the Arts Essential?* (NYU Press, 2022), a collection of essays that explores the intrinsic and instrumental value of the arts in society. The book grew out of a unique multiyear project of research and conferences, which marshaled the contributions of artists, cultural professionals, foundation leaders, and scholars in the arts, humanities, and social sciences. He served as Project Director for "Staging Change: Arts Engagement and Social Wellbeing Amidst Rapid Social Change," funded by the Mellon Foundation and led by researchers from the Social Impact of the Arts Project at the University of Pennsylvania and NYU Brademas Center. He is the author of several reports on international cultural engagement and the role of arts programs in combating Islamophobia. Before joining the NYU Brademas Center, he served as Special Assistant to the Chairman of the National Endowment for Democracy and has worked in publishing and programming at the Council on Foreign Relations and the Carnegie Council on Ethics and International Affairs. He is a member of the Advisory Council of the American Ditchley Foundation. He received a BA in history from NYU.

ELLYN M. TOSCANO is a member of the Advisory Council of the John Brademas Center of New York University. She currently serves as Executive Director of the Hawthornden

Foundation, a private charitable foundation supporting contemporary writers and the literary arts. The Foundation includes an international residential residency program for creative writers at Hawthornden Castle in Midlothian, Scotland; a second residential program at Casa Ecco, on Lake Como in Italy, which also hosts "Conversazioni," private conferences attended by writers and others in the arts; and a nonresidential retreat site in Brooklyn, New York. Before joining Hawthornden, she was the Senior Director for Programming, Partnerships, and Community Engagement at New York University, where she worked to foster programming and partnerships at the intersections of technology, media, and the arts. For over a decade she served as Executive Director of New York University Florence and Director of Villa La Pietra, a 15th-century villa, historic garden, and collection of six thousand objects dating from the Etruscans to the 20th century. She was founder of La Pietra Dialogues, a year-long series of conferences and talks, and founder and producer of The Season, a summer festival that assembled artists, writers, musicians, and public intellectuals to produce new works or reinterpretations of classics in the Villa's expansive Renaissance revival gardens. Prior to NYU, she served as Chief of Staff and Counsel to Congressman Jose Serrano of New York for two decades. Before that she served as Counsel to the New York State Assembly Committee on Education. She is a member of the board of the Civitella Ranieri Foundation and has served on the boards of Federal Hall National Memorial, the Bronx Museum of the Arts, the Brooklyn Academy of Music (as the representative of the Brooklyn Borough President), the Brooklyn Book Festival, and Friends of FAI (Fondo Ambiente Italiano). She served as a Commissioner on the New York City Commission on Gender Equity. A lawyer by training, she earned an LLM in International Law from NYU.

About the Contributors

IMRAN AHMED is the founder and CEO of the Center for Countering Digital Hate. He is an authority on social and psychological malignancies on social media, such as identity-based hate, extremism, disinformation, and conspiracy theories. He appears regularly in the media and documentaries as an expert in how bad actors use digital spaces to harm others and benefit themselves, as well as in how and why bad platforms allow them to do so. Ahmed advises politicians around the world on policy and legislation. He was inspired to start the Center after seeing the rise of antisemitism on the left in the United Kingdom and the murder of his colleague, Jo Cox, MP, by a white supremacist who had been radicalized in part online during the 2016 EU referendum. He holds an MA in Social and Political Sciences from the University of Cambridge.

K. ANTHONY APPIAH is Professor of Law and Philosophy at New York University. A scholar of ethics, political philosophy, and African and African American literary and cultural studies, since 2014 he has taught at NYU's campuses in New York and Abu Dhabi. From 2002 to 2013, he was a member of the Princeton University faculty, and he has also taught at the University of Ghana, Yale, Cornell, Duke, and Harvard. Among his recent books are *Cosmopolitanism: Ethics in a World of Strangers* (W. W. Norton, 2006); *Experiments in Ethics* (Harvard University Press, 2008); *The Honor Code: How Moral Revolutions Happen* (W. W. Norton, 2010); *Lines of Descent: W. E. B. Du Bois and the Emergence of Identity* (Harvard University Press, 2014); and *The Lies That Bind: Rethinking Identity* (Liveright, 2018). In addition to his scholarly work, he writes the weekly column "The Ethicist" for the *New York Times Magazine*.

JULIA AZARI is Associate Professor of Political Science at Marquette University. She holds PhD, MA, and MPhil degrees in political science from Yale University, and a BA in political science from the University of Illinois, Urbana–Champaign. Her research and teaching interests include the American presidency, American political parties, the politics of the American state, and qualitative research methods. Her research has been supported by the Harry Middleton Fellowship in Presidential Studies and the Harry Truman Library Institute Scholars Award. She is a regular contributor at the political science blog Mischiefs of Faction, and her work has also appeared in *The Washington Post's* Monkey Cage blog, Politico, and FiveThirtyEight. She is cohost of the podcast *Politics in Question* and is author of *Delivering the People's Message: The Changing Politics of the Presidential Mandate* (Cornell University Press, 2014).

CATY BORUM is Executive Director of the Center for Media & Social Impact at American University and Provost Associate Professor at AU's School of Communication. She is also the cofounder and codirector, with cultural strategist Mik Moore, of the *Yes, And . . . Laughter Lab* and *YALLfest*, a competitive incubation lab, pitch program, showcase, and festival that lifts up diverse writers and performers creating new comedy about topics that matter. She has authored/coauthored four books about creative entertainment culture and human rights: *The Revolution Will Be Hilarious: Comedy for Social Change and Civic Power* (NYU Press, 2023); *Story Movements: How Documentaries Empower People and Inspire Social Change* (Oxford University Press, 2020); *A Comedian and an Activist Walk into a Bar: The Serious Role of Comedy in Social Justice* (coauthored with Lauren Feldman, foreword by Norman Lear, University of California Press, 2020); and *Radical Reality: Documentary Storytelling and the Global Fight for Social Justice* (co-authored with David Conrad-Pérez, Oxford University Press, 2025).

PAUL CHEUNG is a mission-focused leader with over two decades of experience driving innovation at the intersection of media, technology, and social impact. His career spans leadership roles at major organizations, including the Center for Public Integrity, Knight Foundation, NBC News, the Associated Press, *The Miami Herald*, and *The Wall Street Journal*, where he has championed initiatives in inclusive storytelling, technology adoption, combating misinformation, and fostering organizational change. Cheung serves as a Strategic Advisor for organizations like Hacks/Hackers and the Online News Association, developing strategic frameworks for AI adoption in journalism. He serves on the boards of the Literacy Lab and the Institute for Independent Journalists. A graduate of NYU, with a Sulzberger Fellowship from Columbia University, Cheung brings his perspective as a Chinese immigrant to his work, consistently advocating for inclusive storytelling and cross-cultural understanding in media.

LARRY COHEN served as president of the 600,000-member Communications Workers of America (CWA) from 2005 to 2015, spending nearly all his adult life as a member, organizer, and officer of the union. He was the founding Chair of Jobs with Justice, an organization that brings labor, community, student, and faith voices together at the national and local levels to win improvements in people's lives and shape the public discourse on workers' rights and the economy. He was also the founding Chair of the Democracy Initiative, a coalition of over 50 membership organizations working together to secure voting rights and remove big money from politics. He is a member of the Democratic National Committee and was appointed by Senator Bernie Sanders as Vice Chair of the Unity Reform Commission. On August 25, 2018, DNC members approved major reform proposals related to the 2020 presidential nominating process and national and state party transparency and democracy. He currently chairs the board of Our Revolution, the successor organization to Bernie 2016.

MICKEY EDWARDS is a Visiting Professor and Lecturer in Public and International Affairs at Princeton University. He represented Oklahoma's fifth district in Congress from 1977 to 1993. He served in the House Republican Leadership and was a member of the Appropriations and Budget Committees. He taught for 11 years at Harvard's John F. Kennedy School of Government, where he was the John Quincy Adams Lecturer in Legislative Practice. He has also been a Visiting Lecturer at Harvard Law School and a Visiting Professor at Georgetown University's Public Policy Institute. He is a Director of The Constitution Project, has cochaired task forces on the war power, on judicial independence, and on the constitutional amendment process, and was a member of the American Bar Association Task Force on Presidential Signing Statements. He has been a weekly political commentator on NPR's *All Things Considered* and a weekly opinion columnist for the *Los Angeles Times, Chicago Tribune,* and other major newspapers. He is author or coauthor of three books and is currently writing a book on American conservatism and the Constitution to be published by Oxford University Press.

JONATHAN HAIDT is the Thomas Cooley Professor of Ethical Leadership at New York University's Stern School of Business. His research examines the intuitive foundations of morality, and how morality varies across cultures—including the cultures of progressives, conservatives, and libertarians. His goal is to help people understand each other, live and work near each other, and even learn from each other despite their moral differences. He has cofounded a variety of organizations and collaborations that apply moral and social psychology toward that end, including HeterodoxAcademy.org, OpenMindPlatform.org, and EthicalSystems.org. He is the author of *The Happiness Hypothesis: Finding Modern Truth in Ancient Wisdom* (Basic Books, 2005) and of the *New York Times* bestsellers *The Righteous Mind: Why Good People are Divided by Politics and Religion* (Pantheon, 2012) and *The Coddling of the American Mind: How Good Intentions and Bad Ideas are Setting Up a Generation for Failure* (coauthored with Greg Lukianoff, Penguin, 2018). In 2019 he was inducted into the American Academy of Arts and Sciences, and was chosen by *Prospect* magazine as one of the world's "Top 50 Thinkers."

LYNN MIE ITAGAKI is an award-winning educator and writer who researches and speaks on interracial relations. As an Associate Professor of Literature and Gender Studies at Claremont McKenna College, she is a nationally recognized expert on interracial civility and conflict who has been interviewed by NPR, PBS, *Time*, and other local and national podcasts and radio shows. She regularly speaks about Asian American history, law, and politics with academic and popular audiences. Her research and teaching interests include interracial ethics, intersectional feminism, and 20th and 21st-century US literature by writers of color. Itagaki's book *Civil Racism: The 1992 Los Angeles Rebellion and the Crisis of Racial Burnout* examines the post–civil rights era in terms of the 1992 Los Angeles interracial conflict. Her next book projects examine the aesthetics and politics of the media bystander in the post-9/11 era and race and economics in literature after the Great Recession. She has published essays in law reviews on civility in mainstream politics, LGBTQ+ employment discrimination, disability rights, and the Voting Rights Act. Her analysis of intersectionality's impact on Asian American experiences appears in Jennifer C. Nash and Samantha Pinto's *Routledge Companion to Intersectionalities*. She was a Visiting Professor at Northumbria University, England, and at Saarland University, Germany, and serves as the coeditor for the book series Since 1970: Studies in Contemporary America at the University of Georgia Press.

KAREN JACKSON-WEAVER is Senior Associate Vice President of Global Faculty Engagement and Innovation Advancement at New York University. She is an expert on educational policy, a historian specializing in religion, ethics, and political affairs, and a former Dean-in-Residence at the Blavatnik School of Government at the University of Oxford. She has also served as an academic dean at Princeton University as well as at Harvard University's Kennedy School of Government. She is currently Vice Chair of the Board of Trustees at the Princeton Theological Seminary. She is the former National Series Editor for the Teaching Religious Studies Series produced by Oxford University Press and the American Academy of Religion. Prior to her leadership roles in higher education, she served under three gubernatorial administrations as the Executive Director of the New Jersey Amistad Commission. In this role, she facilitated and led institutes throughout the country and edited two volumes of primary source documents, which culminated in the publications *Reconstruction Reconsidered: The African-American Presence in American History* and the *Amistad Curricular Guide to American History*. She earned her bachelor's degree at Princeton University, master's degree at Harvard University, and PhD in American History from Columbia University, where she was a Kluge Scholar Fellow, Merit Dissertation fellowship winner, and nominee for the university-wide teaching award.

RICARDO ALBERTO MALDONADO is President and Executive Director of the Academy of American Poets. Previously, he served as Codirector of 92NY's Unterberg Poetry Center in New York City. He is the recipient of fellowships from the New York Foundation for the Arts, CantoMundo, Queer|Art|Mentorship, and the T. S. Eliot and Hawthornden Foundations. He is part of El proyecto de la literatura puertorriqueña / The Puerto Rican Literature Project, a forthcoming online database collecting the creative output of Puerto Rican poets in the diaspora and archipelago, developed in partnership with the University of Houston's Recovering the US Hispanic Literary Heritage Program and the Mellon Foundation. Recent collaborations include: "You Are the Prelude," a commission for a new choral and orchestral piece by Puerto Rican composer Angélica Negrón, which was performed at the reopening gala of New York Philharmonic's David Geffen Hall. He was born and raised in Puerto Rico and is the author of *The Life Assignment* (Four Way, 2020), a finalist for the Poetry Society of America's Norma Farber First Book Award, one of *Remezcla's* Best Books by Latina or Latin American Authors, and Silver Medalist for the Juan Felipe Herrera Best Poetry Book Award. He is also the translator of Dinapiera Di Donato's *Colaterales / Collateral* (National Poetry Series/Akashic, 2013) and coeditor of *Puerto Rico en mi corazón* (Anomalous, 2019), a bilingual anthology that raised funds for grassroots recovery efforts in Puerto Rico after Hurricane Maria.

Author of the recent book *Black Software: The Internet & Racial Justice, from the Afronet to Black Lives Matter*, CHARLTON MCILWAIN is Vice Provost for Faculty Development, Pathways & Public Interest Technology at New York University, where he is also Professor of Media, Culture, and Communication at NYU Steinhardt. He works at the intersections of computing technology, race, inequality, and racial justice activism. He has served as an expert witness in landmark US Federal Court cases on reverse redlining/racial targeting in mortgage lending and testified before the US House Committee on Financial Services about the impacts of automation and artificial intelligence on the financial services sector. He is the author of the PolicyLink report "Algorithmic Discrimination: A Framework and Approach to Auditing & Measuring the Impact of Race-Targeted Digital Advertising." He writes regularly for outlets such as *The Guardian*, *Slate*'s Future Tense, and *MIT Technology Review*, about the intersection of race and technology. He is the founder of the Center for Critical Race & Digital Studies, and is Board President at Data & Society Research Institute. He leads NYU's Alliance for Public Interest Technology, is the University's Designee to the Public Interest Technology University Network, and serves on the executive committee as Cochair of the Ethics Committee for the International Panel on the Information Environment.

NORMAN J. ORNSTEIN is Senior Fellow Emeritus at the American Enterprise Institute, where he has studied politics, elections, and the US Congress for more than four decades. In 1980, along with Thomas Mann and Michael Malbin, he created *Vital Statistics on Congress*, a go-to-reference guide updated every two years that provides impartial data for congressional watchers. He previously served as Codirector of the AEI-Brookings Election Reform Project and is an adviser to the Continuity of Government Commission. He has been involved in political reform for decades, including playing a part in the creation of the Congressional Office of Compliance and the House Office of Congressional Ethics. He served as an election analyst for CBS News for thirty years, and also was an on-air election analyst for BBC News. His books include the bestsellers *One Nation After Trump: A Guide for the*

Perplexed, the Disillusioned, the Desperate, and the Not-Yet Deported (St. Martin's, 2017), with E. J. Dionne and Thomas E. Mann; and *It's Even Worse than It Looks: How the American Constitutional System Collided with the New Politics of Extremism* (Basic Books, 2012), with Mann. Through his family foundation named in honor of his late son Matthew, he helped spearhead the documentary *The Definition of Insanity*, about criminal justice and mental illness, which premiered at the Miami Film Festival in March 2020 and aired nationally on PBS on April 14, 2020.

HUSSEIN RASHID is Assistant Dean for Religion and Public Life and a Lecturer at Harvard Divinity School. He has a BA in Middle Eastern Studies from Columbia University, an MA in Theological Studies from Harvard Divinity School, and an MA and PhD in Near Eastern Languages and Cultures, focusing on South and Central Asia, from Harvard University. He is the founder of islamicate L3C, a consultancy focusing on religious literacy and cultural competency. He has worked with a variety of foundations, nonprofits, and governmental agencies for content expertise on religion broadly, with a specialization in Islam. He has previously taught at Barnard College and the New School. His work includes exploring Shi'i justice theology, the interaction between culture and religion, and the role of the arts in conflict mediation. His research focuses on Muslims and American popular culture, with published academic works on Malcolm X, intra-Muslim racism, teaching Shi'ism, Islam, and comics, Sikhs and Islamophobia, Muslims in film, and American Muslim spaces of worship. He served as Content Expert for the Children's Museum of Manhattan's *America to Zanzibar* exhibit. He is a fellow with the Ariane de Rothschild Fellowship in Social Entrepreneurship, the American Muslim Civic Leadership Institute, and the Truman National Security Project. He is a member of the Guild of Future Architects and on the board of Anikaya Dance. He is coeditor of *Ms. Marvel's America: No Normal* (University Press of Mississippi, 2020).

SARAH SOBIERAJ is Professor of Sociology at Tufts University, with expertise in US political culture, extreme incivility, digital abuse and harassment, and the mediated information environment. Her most recent book, *Credible Threat: Attacks Against Women Online and the Future of Democracy,* was honored with the Roderick P. Hart Outstanding Book Award from the National Communication Association's Political Communication Division and the Best Book Award from the American Sociological Association's Section on Communication, Information Technologies, and Media Sociology. Her other books include *The Outrage Industry: Political Opinion Media and the New Incivility* (with J. Berry, Oxford University Press, 2013) and *Soundbitten: The Perils of Media-Centered Political Activism* (New York University Press, 2011). She is editor of the *Oxford Handbook of Digital Media Sociology* (with D. Rohlinger, Oxford University Press, 2022) and *A Crisis of Civility?: Political Discourse and Its Discontents* (with R. Boatright, D. Young, and T. Schaffer, Routledge, 2019). Her research has appeared in journals such as *Information, Communication & Society, Social Problems, PS: Political Science & Politics,* and *Political Communication.* She and her work have been featured in venues such as *The New York Times, The Washington Post, The Boston Globe,* Politico, Vox, CNN, NPR, *American Prospect, National Review,* and *The Atlantic.* She is a member of the National Institute for Civil Discourse's Research Network and is a Faculty Associate with the Berkman Klein Center for Internet & Society at Harvard University.

CATHARINE R. STIMPSON is Dean Emerita of the Graduate School of Arts & Science and University Professor at New York

University. The founding editor of *Signs: Journal of Women in Culture and Society*, she writes about literature, culture, and education. Her most recent essay is in *Are the Arts Essential?* (2022); her most recent project is on the writing of Gertrude Stein. She has also published a novel, *Class Notes* (Times Books, 1979). She has been a University Professor at Rutgers, the State University of New Jersey, where she was Dean of the Graduate School and Vice Provost for Graduate Education. She has taught at Barnard College, where she was also the first Director of its Women's Center. Her public service has included the chairs of the New York State Council for the Humanities, the National Council for Research on Women, the *Ms. Magazine* Board of Scholars, Creative Capital, and Scholars at Risk. She has served as Director of the Fellows Program at the MacArthur Foundation in Chicago. In 1990, she was President of the Modern Language Association. She has won Fulbright and Rockefeller Humanities Fellowships.

Index

Page numbers in *italics* indicate Figures.